India provided Britain with a volunteer army almost equal in numbers to the combined forces contributed by the dominions of Canada, Australia, New Zealand, and South Africa. Nearly every sixth soldier fighting on behalf of the British Empire would come from the Indian subcontinent. During the war, Indians saw active service not just on the Western Front, but also in the Middle East, Africa and even China.

1. Western Front (1914-18)
2. Italian Campaign (1917-18)
3. Macedonian Front (1915-18)
4. Gallipoli Campaign (1915-16)
5. North Africa Campaign (1915-16)
6. Sinai & Palestine Campaign (1915-18)
7. Persian Campaign (1914-18)
8. Mesopotamian Campaign (1914-20)
9. South Arabian Campaign (1914-19)
10. North-West Frontier Province (1914-18)
11. Russian Operations (1918-19)
12. East African Campaign (1914-18)
13. China Operations (1914)

'If I die here, who will remember me?'

India and the First World War

FOREWORD BY AMITAV GHOSH

'If I die here, who will remember me?'

India and the First World War

VEDICA KANT

Lustre Press
Roli Books

Acknowledgements

I would like to express the deepest gratitude and thanks to a very large number of people without whose help, support, and encouragement this book would not have been possible.

No amount of thanks to the Roli Books team will be enough, and I shall always be grateful to them for giving me the opportunity to work on this project. Even as I express my gratitude to Pramod, Kiran, and Priya Kapoor, I know that this is not enough acknowledgement for the time and effort they have put into this project. They all became the First World War researchers along with me, visiting archives and exhibitions on my behalf, sorting through photographic materials and putting together the visual material that makes this book what it is. They were always available for phone calls and their constant stream of ideas, comments, and critiques have helped no end in bettering the book. Finally, I cannot thank the Roli team enough – especially Sneha Pamneja and Saloni Vaid – for doing such a wonderful job with the design of book and making it look so special.

I am hugely indebted to Amitav Ghosh for encouraging my interest in some of the themes this book explores and for offering me an early opportunity to write on them for his blog. Amitav very kindly agreed to write a foreword to this book, and provided extremely valuable comments and critiques for which I am incredibly grateful.

My interest in India's role in the First World War grew as a tangential interest from researching the various fronts the Ottoman Empire fought on during the war. For that in itself, I owe a huge debt to my academic institutions, St Antony's College and the Middle East Centre at Oxford. I am grateful to my tutors Eugene Rogan, Celia Kerslake, and Laurent Mignon. I would also like to thank Faisal Devji for being a constant source of advice and encouragement.

I have benefited from the help of a number of scholars and institutions during the course of researching this book. Santanu Das has been extremely generous in discussing matters related to India and the First World War, and I shall be forever grateful for the enormous benefit of his scholarly awareness. I am also grateful to Squadron Leader Rana Chhina, Peter Stanley, and Mesut Uyar for discussing various aspects of the war with me.

Archivists and staff at various libraries and archives have shared their knowledge and helped with the making of this book. I am grateful to Penny Brooke, Antonia Moon, John Falconer, and John O'Brien at the British Library; Parveen Sodhi and Suzanne Bardgett at the Imperial War Museum; and Tess Hines at the Mary Evans Picture Library.

Ronny Gobyn and Hilde Lauwaert were extremely kind and gracious hosts in Belgium. They tirelessly drove us through the battlefields of France and Flanders, and a lot of this book would not have been possible without their help. Dominiek Dendooven, Annick Vandenbilcke, Piet Chielens, and the staff of the In Flanders Field Museum were beyond helpful in identifying useful materials and contacts, and I am hugely thankful for their help. I would also like to thank Capt. Christophe Cazorla and Sgt Nicolas Nacher at the French Military archives for their help in identifying valuable materials. I am also grateful to Shivanand and Sneha Sinha for their hospitality in Brussels.

Dominique Faivre grew up hearing his grandmother's stories about Indian soldiers billeted in France and this spurred his interest in collecting First World War-era Indian Army images and materials. Dominique has been incredibly gracious in allowing us the use of his vast collection, and I cannot thank him enough for his generosity.

Mishka Sinha hosted me in Berlin and I am grateful to her for being a wonderful guide to the city. I am also grateful to Heike Leibau, Franziska Roy, and Larissa Schmid at the Zentrum Modern Orient for their willingness to share information about Indian POWs in Germany. Britta Lange was extremely kind to invite me to her exhibition 'The Making of... Ghosts: Voices and Apparitions in the Archives of the First World War' and to point out material that would be useful for the book. Sarah Gossert was extremely helpful and patient in guiding me through the collection of Humboldt University's Lautarchiv. I would also like to thank Maik Lamolla for showing me around the town of Wünsdorf and sharing a number of images of Indian POWs, and would also like to thank the Museum of European Cultures.

Kerem Tinaz and his family adopted me during my time in Istanbul, for which no amount of thanks will suffice. I am grateful to Semanur Karaman, Elizabeth Angell, Timur Hammond, Husseyin Ege, and Atiya Yalcin Ege, Nick Danforth, and Chris Gratien for being friends and family to me and making the time I spent in Istanbul extremely special. Layli Uddin, Richard Williams, Supriya Nair, Aparna Kapadia, Ekin Oklap, and Ramata Hoorntjee have been wonderful friends and colleagues whose help and support I am extremely lucky to have. Robert Upton was kind enough to read and comment on everything I sent his way. He has been a constant source of knowledge and support and helped no end in editing the book and suggesting titles for it – I could not be more grateful.

I would like to thank my extended family for all their love and support. I owe a special thank you to my cousin Richa Roy, who was kind enough to read multiple drafts of the book and provide invaluable comments and feedback. Saying thank you to my parents and my sister is only a small acknowledgement for their constant love and encouragement. They have been an unending source of strength and support throughout this whole process and for that I will be forever grateful.

Contents

Facing page: An Indian cavalry brigade at work in rural France.

A wounded officer of the Indian Army is pictured in the grounds of the hospital at Brighton, holding the helmet of a German officer, which he had captured at Neuve Chapelle.

Foreword

Of the many poignant images in this book, none captures better the plight of the colonial soldier than the photograph (on p. 171) in which a sepoy in a prisoner-of-war camp is seen to be washing his foot while a German soldier looks on, bemused, from the other side of a barbed-wire fence. Whether in captivity or not, the sepoy had always to contend with the gaze of those he served: on the other side of the battle-lines too he would have known himself to be under constant watch, hemmed in by fences that related not only to his physical being but most significantly to the question of his loyalty, this last being a matter of such profound uncertainty that no one perhaps was more unsure of it than he himself. It is this ambivalence above all, that defines the predicament of the sepoy, not just in the First World War, but in many other conflicts before and after.

The sepoy's way of soldiering dated back to a time when mercenary armies were the norm rather than the exception – that is to say, the mid-18th century, which was when the East India Company raised its first 'Native Infantry' regiments in the newly-founded Presidencies of Bombay, Madras and Bengal. The First World War sepoy is thus the embodiment of a paradox: a soldier schooled in modern weaponry and tactics but recruited, remunerated and officered by methods that belonged to another era. The sepoy was in other words a warrior of a completely different ilk from the citizen-soldiers who were the main protagonists of the First World War: this is one reason why his role in that conflict is so often overlooked, at home and in the West.

Since the creation of the East India Company's standing armies, the sepoy had fought in innumerable British campaigns in Asia and Africa through the Mysore Wars, the Maratha Wars, the Opium Wars, and so on. Yet, across those centuries of service one thing that remained constant was the sepoy's ambivalent relationship to his job. His loyalty could never be taken for granted; mutiny, which always simmered beneath the surface, regularly came to the boil, most spectacularly in 1857. Nor did his ambivalence end with the start of First World War: sepoys mutinied at Singapore in 1915 even as their compatriots were fighting side-by-side with English regiments at the Somme; a generation later the story would repeat itself on a much larger scale, in the same theatre, during the Second World War. This split in the sepoy's loyalties is perfectly captured in Vedica Kant's account (pp. 121-23) of two Afridi Pathan brothers, one of whom Mir Dast, won the Victoria Cross at Ypres, while the other, Mir Mast, deserted to the German side at Neuve Chapelle, along with 24 other sepoys.[1]

This is why the Indian[2] soldier's experience of the First World War resists appropriation by those who would like to merge it seamlessly into the triumphal narrative of the winning side. The sepoy's ambivalence, as much as the anomalous circumstances of the army to which he belonged, made sure that his story could not be fitted into the usual frames of 'victor' and 'vanquished'. This is another reason why the sepoy's role in the war is so often overlooked.

In a sense, the sepoy was himself complicit in this neglect – for not the least aspect of his ambivalence was his witholding of his own story. Through the history of his existence, silence was one of the sepoy's most enduring traits; it goes so far back and is so consistent that it is hard not to see it as an act of resistance in itself. Consider that in the century and a half that preceded the First World War hundreds of thousands of Indians, many of them literate, served as sepoys. Yet over that entire period there exists only one first person narrative of a sepoy's experiences, and this too is possibly an apocryphal text: *Sitaram Subedar.*[3]

Nor did the First World War, which was to result in an enormous outpouring of prose and poetry in English, French and German, have a similar effect on the Indian subcontinent. While Europe produced tens of thousands of books about the war, in India only a tiny number of first person accounts were to find their way into print: to date they can still be counted on the fingers of one hand – and not one of them was written by a sepoy.

In fact two of these accounts were written by men who were not even eligible to serve as sepoys by reason of their ethnicity; they were Bengalis and thus excluded from military recruitment because of the British Indian army's racial policies.[4] One of these men, Kalyan Mukherjee, was a doctor in the army's medical corps, the other, Sisir Sarbadhikari, was a medical auxiliary.[5] Although neither of them bore arms, their writings are to my mind, among the most remarkable accounts of the violence of the First World War. This is of course a tall claim to make of a conflict that was so fecund in literary production: since neither of the two books has been translated, I am afraid the only substantiation I can provide, for those who do not read Bengali, is the evidence of the excerpts that I have translated for my own blog (several passages of which are included in this book).[6]

As for the sepoys themselves, true to their tradition, they left behind very little: inasmuch as their voice can be heard at all it is through their censored letters,[7] and through the various materials that were collected by scholars in German prisoner-of-war camps.[8] These sources have only recently seen the light of day and this book is one of the first to incorporate them into a panoramic overview of the Indian subcontinent's involvement in the First World War. It is a welcome and long-necessary endeavour but it should be noted that on certain subjects there remains a yawning gap in information: for example the role of lascars, who probably contributed more, proportionally, to the seaborne war effort than sepoys did on land.

Despite the gaps in the record, Vedica Kant has succeeded, to a quite remarkable degree, in conveying a sense of the texture of the sepoy's experience and of the conflicted, ambivalent cadences of his voice. It is a voice that cries out to be heard, precisely because its story does not conform to the mirrored Western narratives of victory and defeat: what it offers is the possibility of an alternative reading of that history – as a story both of defeat-in-victory and victory-in-defeat. To my mind this is closer to the truth of what happened on the battlefields of Europe and Asia during the First World War than many more familiar interpretations of those tragic events.

Amitav Ghosh
August 2014

A French war-era postcard portrays 'Mysterious India' on the side of England in the defence of civilization.

THE WAR

Nelson's Picture Weekly

No. 11 October 31, 1914

A Sikh soldier trying to learn the French language.

The War: Nelson's Picture Weekly was a British publication that gave illustrated news of the war to a wide audience. Many Britons saw the war years as a landmark in Britain's relationship with its colonies and there was an upswing of awareness and celebration of Britain's colonial connections. The war was important for its cultural and political ramifications, exposing Indian soldiers to ways of life very different from their own.

A Call to Duty

India and the First World War

It must not be imagined that I have any illusions as to the part played by the Indians, as will be made clear throughout this book. No one knows better than I do how utterly impossible it would have been for them to do what they did, without the help and example of their illustrious comrades of the Scotch, Irish, and English battalions which formed part of each brigade, or of the splendid territorial units which later joined us, and the superb British Artillery which paved the way for all our efforts. But of these History will assuredly furnish a brilliant account. It is not always so of Indian troops; their raconteurs are few and far between; the chief actors in the play, still living, will probably be counted by tens not thousands. The rank and file will furnish no writers to thrill the generations to come; they will just pass with the great masses of India, content that they have done their duty and been faithful to their salt.

General Sir James Willcocks, Commander of the Indian Corps in France during the First World War [1]

+++

It was my good fortune to be engaged in this war. We shall never get such another chance to exalt the name of race, country, ancestors, parents, village and brothers, and to prove our loyalty to the Government. Do not be distressed... Such hardships come upon brave men. What is fated must be endured. I pray to God to give us a chance to meet the foe face to face... To die in battle is a noble fate. I expect we shall get our chance. When we go to the trenches we go in such spirits as to the wedding of a younger brother, or like boys to a fair. We go singing as we march and care nothing that we are going to die. The fighting is strange – on the ground, in the sky and in the sea, everywhere. This is rightly called the war of kings. We have seen many things of which we cannot write. If we return alive, I will tell you all about it.

Signaller Kartar Singh (France) to Kunar Khan (Ludhiana District, Punjab)[2]

+++

On 28 June 1914, a Serbian nationalist in Sarajevo assassinated Franz Ferdinand, the Archduke of Austria-Hungary along with his pregnant wife, Sofia. The event did not initially raise many eyebrows in the capitals of Europe – the Balkans were known to be prone to instability and radical politics, after all. And yet, within a month, this seemingly local matter between Austria and its irredentist neighbour Serbia had bewilderingly turned into the First World War.

A hundred years later, historians still debate and ponder the ways in which the assassination of one couple led to a global war that was characterized by an unholy combination of industrial savagery and slow attrition that went on for four long years and left few parts of the world truly unaffected.

Europe was the source and the centre of the conflict, but given the vast empires of many European states and the fact that the war also became one about imperial control, it is hardly surprising that it engulfed large swathes of the world. As the historian Hew Strachan has noted, 'war for Europe meant war for the world'.[3] If the war was a strange and surprising outcome for Europe, it was perhaps even more so for many of the colonial troops who were quickly drafted into fighting on behalf of their imperial masters and found themselves engaged in various battles across a variety of fronts.

A forgotten colonial war

When the war broke out, Great Britain and France had the two largest colonial empires in the world and both relied extensively on their colonies for manpower, material, and infrastructure. Britain relied heavily on the Indian Army and India more generally for the war effort, but there were also contributions by the other British colonies – Canada, Australia, New Zealand, Newfoundland and South Africa. France recruited troops from West Africa, Madagascar, Algeria, Tunisia, Morocco and Indo-China. So multicultural and multiracial was the war that the German sociologist Max Weber took to saying that the Entente armies were comprised of 'niggers, Gurkhas, and the barbarians of the world'.[4] Over the four years of the war, fighting would take place not just in Europe, but also Africa (which was completely under European rule with the exception of Ethiopia and Liberia), the Middle East, Central Asia and the Far East, with Indians fighting on many of these fronts. By one estimate, every sixth soldier sent into the war by the British Empire came from the Indian subcontinent.[5] However, as Willcocks seemed to rightly portend, a combination of Eurocentrism and unease about the imperial past has meant this aspect of the war has received fairly little popular attention.

Left to right: Coloured postcards show soldiers of the 5th Gurkha Rifles, 3rd Sappers and Miners and 26th King George's Own (Light Cavalry); 43rd Erinpura Regiment, 44th Merwara Regiment, 108th Infantry; a soldier identified as 'Rajput'; Maharaja Ganga Singh of Bikaner who commanded the Bikaner Camel Corps during the war. He was the only non-white member of the British Imperial War Cabinet and represented India at the 1919 Paris Peace Conference.

For a soldier in India in June 1914, the idea of being deployed to a war abroad would have been a far thought. How many of them would have known who Franz Ferdinand was or what had led to the British Empire embarking on this war against the Germans and Austrians is questionable. Sisir Sarbadhikari, a Bengali who served with the voluntary Bengal Ambulance Corps in Mesopotamia during the war, wrote in his memoirs about how he first reacted to news of Franz Ferdinand's assassination:

> When we first heard the news none of us were particularly interested. Who cared where Sarajevo was and which Archduke had been assassinated there? We barely took the trouble to look at the reports in the newspapers. We thought it was just a little bit of bother that would soon be sorted out.[6]

And yet, by August 1914, hundreds of thousands of Indians – not just as infantry and cavalry, but also sappers, miners and followers – were making their way for the first time across the *kala pani,* the black waters that Hindus had for centuries been forbidden to cross for fear of losing caste, to take their part in the war. They initially fought on the Western Front (the first time Indian troops were deployed in Europe) and then in the Middle East and East Africa as well. British India (comprising India, Pakistan, Bangladesh, Sri Lanka and Burma) and Nepal (which contributed troops to the Indian Army) made the largest contribution to the war effort in terms of manpower of any of the colonies and dominions of the British Empire, with almost one and a half million Indians participating in the war.[7] There is still no final confirmation of the number of Indian dead. Best estimates put the figure above 70,000.[8] In monetary terms, India contributed £100 million outright in 1914 (approximately £8 billion in today's value) and another £20 to £30 million (roughly £1.6 to £2.4 billion today) each year in cash thereafter for the war.[9] India also provided over 170,000 animals and 3,700,000 tons of supplies and stores to support the war effort.[10] It is worth questioning, even a hundred years later, what effect Britain's ability to leverage these colonial resources had in the final outcome of a long, exhausting, struggle that demanded a constant stream of men to be sent to the frontlines.

Left to right: 1st Duke of York's Own Lancers, 3rd Skinner's Horse; Mysore Transport Corps and the Mysore Lancers; 14th Murray's Jat Lancers; 37th Lancers (Baluch Horse), 36th Jacob's Lancers; 35th Scinde Horse.

Despite the Indian contribution, there is limited existent memory or understanding of the scale and nature of this involvement, or of ordinary soldiers' experience of the war in India itself. One of Delhi, and indeed India's, most celebrated monuments, the India Gate, is dedicated to the 'dead of the Indian armies who fell honoured in France and Flanders, Mesopotamia, and Persia, East Africa, Gallipoli and elsewhere in the Near and Far East in 1914–1918 war'. Tourists flock to the site today, but most would be surprised to learn that the memorial was built and inaugurated by the British in 1931 to honour the soldiers who died in these far off places. The Amar Jawan Jyoti, which was added to the site following the 1971 Bangladesh Liberation War in memory of the unknown Indian

The iconic India Gate, located in the heart of New Delhi was built by the British to commemorate the Indian war dead, a fact that might be surprising to many of its visitors today.

soldier, was a refashioning of the symbolism of the site away from its colonial legacy. India Gate remains the iconic site the British wanted it to be, but today it stands largely stripped of its intended meaning and context.

On the occasion of the centennial of the war, it is worth asking if India's role in the war is worth remembering after all. At a panel discussion on the war at a literary festival on a cold January morning in 2014, an audience member pointedly stated that any talk about remembering the contribution of soldiers from the subcontinent to the war effort was ill-conceived. These soldiers were mere mercenaries; their efforts misplaced in their fighting *for* rather than *against* the colonial authorities. This is not a surprising point of view. In the post-colonial, nationalist milieu of a country that has become free of colonialism the memorialisation of soldiers who fought for an imperial cause is an uncomfortable reminder of the complex and intertwined histories that bound India and its colonial master.

It is this complexity that makes the war a crucial episode in Indian history. The war deserves further engagement precisely because of its impact on India. For one, it is important to recognize the importance of the war on India's national politics at the time and on the anti-colonial struggle itself. When the war broke out, numerous nationalist leaders in India (including Mahatma Gandhi, Bal Gangadhar Tilak, and Sarojini Naidu amongst others) pushed for Indians to take on a large role in the war. To some extent at least this reflected a genuine belief that it was in India's interests to fight Germany and her allies for the sake of her own security. The bombardment of Madras by the German cruiser *SMS Emden* in September 1914 only made such fears more acute.

Many nationalist leaders also campaigned extensively for the war effort because they believed that India's contribution to the war would allow her to demand greater freedoms from Great Britain. This is not as surprising as it might seem today. The trajectory of the Indian freedom struggle was not a simple, constant demand for independence that it is often assumed to be. When the war broke out, the demands of a large section of the Indian political elite were for home rule and a style of government similar to Britain's white dominions, and they believed that India could use her role in the war as a bargaining chip to fulfil these demands. As Bal Gangadhar Tilak took to saying, 'Purchase war debentures but look at them as title deeds of Home Rule.'[11] There was some political reward for this support when in August 1917 Edwin Montagu, the Secretary of State for India, announced that British policy in India was now aimed at 'increasing association of Indians in every branch of the administration, and the gradual

Regimental badges of units involved in the war effort. From left to right: the 18th Infantry, 62nd Punjabis, 9th Bhopal Infantry, and the 129th Duke of Connaught's Own Baluchis.

development of self-governing institutions, with a view to the progressive realization of responsible government in India as an integral part of the British Empire.' The declaration gave nationalists in India a clear goal to now work towards and made it difficult for the British to backtrack on these promises without the prospect of mass discontent and disorder.

It is not only for its impact on the course of Indian politics in the run up to independence that the Indian involvement in the war needs reconsideration, but also for the very personal impacts that the war had on the soldiers and non-combatants from India who participated in it. The almost unquenchable thirst for manpower caused by the war had much broader ramifications than just those on the soldier classes who were frequently recruited from the so-called martial races and now found themselves battling for the Empire abroad. In addition to a constant need for troops there was also a need for auxiliary servicemen such as labourers, porters, the mule drivers who brought in ammunition, cooks, stretcher bearers or even the *bhisti*, who slaked soldiers' thirst. To supply this need for manpower, the Government of India reached out into a number of tribal communities across Assam, Manipur, Burma, Bihar, and Orissa in addition to also exporting prison labour to the war fronts.[12] All these men were exposed to the full horrors of the war, whose industrialized nature distinguished it from those that preceded it and blurred the boundaries between combatants and non-combatants.

Santanu Das, the preeminent scholar of the Indian experience in the Great War, has noted that the dire need for manpower during the war led to a stark and grotesque reversal of the vision from Joseph Conrad's *Heart of Darkness,* as hundreds of thousands of brown men journeyed to the heart of Empire.[13] The war opened up new spaces, opportunities, and levels of contact and interaction for Indians not just with Europe and Europeans, but also other parts of the world. It is also important, then, to remember the war as a strange moment when many of the rules of colonialism were suspended and to try and imagine what impact this experience had on those who had to negotiate these complicated and nebulous boundaries.

The home front was not spared either, feeling the impact of the war most acutely through a diversion of economic resources for the war effort. The infrastructure provided by India – railways, docks, harbour-works, plantations, mining

complexes, oil fields and rubber plantations – was crucial to Britain's military needs at the time. In addition, India was an important partner in bearing some of the costs of the war. The Indian taxpayer funded the Indian Army and India was an important market for war bonds. India so completely took on the costs of the war that even Prisoners of War (POWs) from fronts in Mesopotamia and East Africa were sent to POW camps in India at an expense to the Indian taxpayer. The shortages and price rises that occurred during the war years were sharply felt by ordinary Indians and were the catalyst of the civil disorder that marked Indian politics in the aftermath of the war in what was to be perhaps the most challenging period of rule for the British in India since the 1857 revolt.

The strange gap in India's historical memory about the war years might suggest that post-war political agitations were a natural development in India's march to independence and had little to do with India's involvement in the war. However, they were very much a result of the frustrations that many Indians, both at the level of national politics and as former combatants, felt at the raw deal they had received from the British after years of supporting and participating in the war effort.

The national politics of war

British India had for decades been a reservoir of cheap military labour available to be used by the imperial authorities, an 'English barrack in the Oriental seas'.[14] Unsurprisingly, when the war broke out in August 1914, the only overseas troops immediately available for deployment were those of the Indian Army. For India, the First World War came at a strange time. The nation was caught at a moment of growing nationalism, as evidenced by the swadeshi movement, that had nevertheless not yet reached such proportions as to snap the country's loyalty to the Raj.[15] As a result, when the King sent his message asking the 'Princes and People of My Indian Empire' to support the war

Facing page and above: During their time in France the Indian troops caught the attention of a local French artist Paul Sarrut who spent time observing and sketching the men as they went about their daily activities, both military and the very quotidian.

effort the response was extremely enthusiastic – not just from the Indian princely states, but also the political bourgeoisie.

The British War Council agreed upon the Indian involvement in the war as early as 5 August 1914. Fighting imperial campaigns was not new for the Indian Army. It had previously fought not just on the Northwest frontiers of India, but also in places like China, Abyssinia, Perak, Egypt and Sudan. However, this was an important moment in the army's history because it opened up the possibility of service in Europe. The deployment of Indian troops in Europe had thus far been avoided because the British were concerned about upholding 'white prestige'. It was for this reason that the British had avoided using the Indian Army when in conflict with white enemies such as in the Boer War of 1899-1902. Having Indians kill white men in the battlefield could, after all, potentially upset the strict racial hierarchies and threaten the colonial machinery. Having had the experience of killing white men in the battlefield what would stop the Indian soldiers from thinking that they could turn on their masters? Still, necessity triumphed over ideology. Hardinge was keen to satisfy what he perceived as 'advanced' (that is, more politically demanding) Indian opinion that wanted greater involvement in the war, and urged an end to the colour bar that prevented Indian troops from serving in Europe. It was a position the King also came out in support of.

Once war had been declared, the mobilisation of troops began. By the end of the month, with the British troops on the Western Front suffering heavy setbacks, the war council decided that four Indian divisions, which formed Indian Expeditionary Force A, would be sent to the battlefields of Europe

Indian troops were drafted into the war as early as August 1914. Over the next four years, Indian troops would see action as far afield as northern France, the Middle East, East Africa, and even China. Here Indian troops at Dar-es-Salaam embark for Kilwa in October 1917.

D.19-16

as reinforcement.[16] At the same time smaller Expeditionary Forces B, C, and D were also being assembled for deployment in East Africa and Mesopotamia. In September 1914, the first Indian troops began reaching the scene of battle; they landed in Marseilles still in their tropical uniforms. The deployment of Indian soldiers to the war was met by a wave of celebratory remarks in newspapers in Britain. Perhaps the early months of the war were ripe to create a moment of sentimentality at the Empire coming together to fight the enemy. In a speech at the Indian Empire Club, the former Viceroy Lord Curzon described the arrival of the Indians as a 'dramatic moment in the history of the Indian Empire' and as a 'landmark in our connection with India'.[17]

In India too, a similar sentiment held sway as princely rulers and political leaders attempted to make the most of the opportunity offered by the war. For the various princely states (who still ruled about one-third of India in partnership with the Raj), the War was an opportunity to ingratiate themselves with the British. The Imperial Service Troops, forces raised by the princely states of the British Empire, were quickly placed at the disposal of the Viceroy. The 700-odd native princes also

One reason the Indian war experience is today largely forgotten is the lack of first-person accounts from the soldiers themselves. While a number of soldiers were literate, educational attainment in the Indian Army was uneven at best, thus making, a hundred years after the war, the voice of the Indian soldier hard to hear. Here, an illiterate Indian soldier of the 7th (Meerut) Division, makes a thumb impression on his pay sheet instead of signing his name for his pay.

started to compete with each other with their offers of troops, money, and war goods. Sir Pertab Singh, the Regent of Jodhpur and other prominent leaders from states like Bikaner and Patiala volunteered to go to the front. The Maharaja of Mysore made a contribution of Rs.50 lakhs, the Maharaja of Baroda, Rs.5 lakhs. Gwalior offered an interest-free loan of Rs.50 lakhs in addition to troops, labourers, hospital ships, ambulances, motorcars, flotillas, horses, materials, food and clothes. The Begum of Bhopal sent 500 copies of the Koran and 1,487 copies of other religious tracts for Muslim soldiers. The Maharaja of Patiala sent *romals* to spread on the Adi Granth and *chanani* to Sikh soldiers in Germany. The Nizam of Hyderabad made a particularly munificent offer of six million rupees for the maintenance of two cavalry units in France. Even the smaller landlords and chieftains were not to be left behind – the Thakur of Bagli, for example, donated socks, shirts, mufflers, tobacco, cigarettes and chocolates for the Indian troops in East Africa, Mesopotamia and Egypt.[18]

Leaders such as the Nizam of Hyderabad, the Nawab of Palanpur, the Begum of Bhopal, and Aga Khan also spoke publicly about the need for continuing loyalty from their subjects towards the British. This loyal support for the British cause became especially significant with the Ottoman Empire joining the War on the side of the Germans on 28 October 1914. The Ottoman Sultan was also considered the *khalifa* or religious leader by most South Asian Muslims and the presence of a large number of Muslim soldiers in the Indian Army raised British fears of desertion or worse, jihad, if these troops were made to fight against their Turkish religious brethren.[19] An example of this continuing loyalty can be seen in the Begum of Bhopal's speech at the Delhi War Conference in April 1918, where she stressed that, 'Now that the war has entered upon a more intense phase we assure you that it will never be said that in this supreme crisis India when weighed in balance was found wanting.'[20] The British did recognize this outpouring of loyalty by the princely states – for example, the Nizam of Hyderabad was bestowed with the title 'His Exalted Highness'. The famous Teen Murti statue that gave the Teen Murti Bhavan, (famous as the residence of the Commander-in-Chief of the Indian Army and later the Prime Minister of India, Jawaharlal Nehru) its name was built in 1922 in memory of the Indian soldiers from the princely states of Jodhpur, Hyderabad and Mysore who served in Palestine during the War.

Like the princely states, the nationalists of the time also had a vested interest in supporting the war effort, even if their motives were significantly different. The Indian National Congress pledged its support to the Allied cause and a number of other parties, including the All India Muslim League, agreed. Some of the leading political figures of the time campaigned extensively for the war effort and to boost recruitment. Such a response was partly built on the calculation that India's strong role in the war would lead to political pay-offs. Indeed, as Annie Beasant, who had founded the India Home Rule League in 1916 wrote: 'When the war is over... we cannot doubt that the King-Emperor will, as reward for her glorious defence of the Empire, pin upon her breast the jewelled medal of Self-Government within the Empire.'[21] It is important to note this emphasis on self-government within the confines of Empire, which made supporting Britain's war aims doubly important. As the Tamil nationalist poet Subramania Bharthi wrote, 'We want Home Rule. We advocate no violence. We shall always adopt peaceful and legal methods... In peace time we shall be uncompromising critics of England's mistakes. But when trouble comes we shall unhesitatingly stand by her, and if necessary, defend her against her enemies.'[22] Even Mahatma Gandhi who was at the time in London, en route to India after his South African sojourn, noted at the beginning of the war that he thought that 'England's need should not be turned into our opportunity and that it was more becoming and far-sighted not to press our demands while the war lasted.'[23]

But there was also another factor at play.

Service in the war was seen by many Indians as a way to establish racial equality by proving that Indians were not lacking in courage or loyalty. The British recruited largely according to the so-called 'Martial Races Theory', which had at its core the belief that some Indians were inherently more warlike, bringing together indigenous notions of caste and the ideas of Social Darwinism. Few troops were recruited from eastern and southern India or urban areas because of the detrimental effects of 'racial degeneracy'. The Western-educated were also excluded for their possibly politically subversive potential. The period of the war was marked by vociferous lobbying for the inclusion of a wider spectrum of Indians into the army. In particular, there was a constant demand to open up the officer ranks of the army to Indians by allowing them to become King's Commissioned Officers (KCOs), which would enable them to take on official duties equivalent to a white officer. More broadly it was hoped that the need for men during the war would provide the opportunity to recapture martiality and martial traditions among non-martial Indians. While KCOs were not granted to Indians, the need for men as the war progressed led to recruitment out of necessity from not just non-martial communities but also marginalized and outcast communities such as tribals and untouchables.

For Bal Gangadhar Tilak, this broadening of recruitment offered many Indians the opportunity for military training that had so far been denied to them and was seen as a valuable instruction for the defence of India. Mahatma Gandhi, too, eventually came around to unconditional advocacy of enlistment (a position the historian Judith Brown had described as 'a strange phenomenon for one who preached non-violence').[24] Writing an 'Appeal for Enlistment' leaflet, Gandhi wrote: 'To bring about such a state of things we should have the ability to defend ourselves, that is, the ability to bear arms and to use them... If we want to learn the use of arms with the greatest possible dispatch, it is our duty to enlist ourselves in the army.' For Gandhi, 'Home Rule without military power was useless, and this was the best opportunity to get it'. An India 'trained for fighting will be able to wrest freedom in a moment', and with the strength gained on the battlefield 'even fight the Empire, should it

Postcards from the war depict the Pioneer Regiments and (right) the 46th and 33rd Punjabis.

play foul with us'.[25] This idea of the military service somehow bettering the Indian people was also taken up by the Congresswoman Sarojini Naidu, who wrote 'Let young Indians, who are ready to die for India and to wipe from her bow the brand of slavery, rush to join the standing army, or to be more correct, India's citizen army composed of cultured young men, of young men of tradition and ideals, men who burn with the shame of slavery in the hearts.'[26]

Understanding this political milieu in India during the war can perhaps help one understand how easy it might have been for individual sepoys to get caught up in the fervour of war and how this might have been just as important a motivation in fighting as any economic benefit that would be accrued. Like most initial volunteers across the world, the war might have initially seemed a great adventure. They would get the chance to see *vilayat*, to meet people from other cultures, to fight alongside European soldiers. Some of the journeys the soldiers made would seem fantastic to people in India even today and one can only imagine just what a life-changing (and in some tragic instances, life-ending) journey this must have been for the more than a million Indians who experienced the war.

The personal politics of war

It would not be an overestimation to say that the war was a transformational, perhaps even a defining moment, for all those involved at the front. What this experience was like for Indian troops, how they reacted to the situations they found themselves in,

A war-era postcard of troops from the British Empire shows the Indian contingent dressed in all their regimental finery.

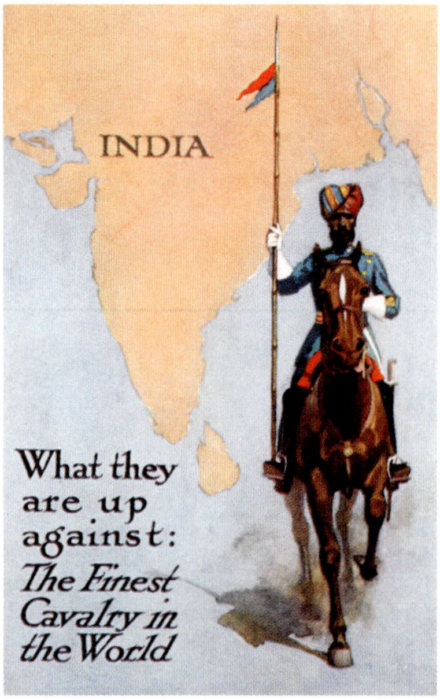

and the impact this had on the colonial relationship is an underexplored subject. This is partly because we have few detailed first-hand accounts of their war experiences. In 1914, the Indian Army largely comprised troops who were quite often semi-literate and did not leave behind a body of work that would viscerally bring alive the war for generations to come.

The First World War was a moment of all sorts of strange transcultural encounters that were not just limited to the battlefield. The war made Indians a familiar feature in the theatres of war. In his diaries Siegfried Sassoon, the great English war poet, noted: 'I watched the Indian cavalry in the horse-lines by the river: their red head-caps made occasional spots of colour.'[27] Wilfred Owen, along with Sassoon another leading English war poet, scribbled in his trench notebook a text by Tagore, 'When I go from hence let this be my parting word, that what I have seen is unsurpassable'.[28] After his death his mother wrote to the great poet to say how moved her son had been by the lines. Despite their immense presence on the battlefields the Indian experiences of the time have been largely haunted by a ghostly silence. The memories of the war still linger in families and army regiments, but while the experience of war probably had a lasting impact on the lives of those on the frontline they did not lead to any broader discourse on what motivated these soldiers to fight or how their war experiences impacted their view of the world.

Despite the lack of cohesive, organized materials one can start piecing together from these fragments what the war years were like for a vast majority of Indians and how these experiences influenced and shaped the atmosphere in India itself during this period. What were their motivations to fight? What was it like to cross the *kala pani* to a foreign land? What did they make

Postcards of the time celebrated, with humour and colonial pride, the Indian contribution to the Allied war effort. From left to right: A postcard declared the Indian cavalry the finest in the world; 'The German elephant has found its mahout' stated another showing an Indian soldier riding an injured and disabled elephant; India is ready and willing to put her troops in service of John Bull, the personification of Britain, implied the third.

The Martial Races Theory

The make-up of the Indian Army on the eve of the outbreak of the First World War was largely restricted to certain social groups. This was primarily a function of the Indian Army's policy of recruiting from only certain geographical areas of the country whose 'races' were considered the most 'martial'.

The main argument of the theory was quite simply that not all Indians were equal in soldierly qualities – some races were superior to others. The martial races theory gained traction as a legitimate theory to guide army recruitment at a time when social Darwinist racial theories were increasingly popular in Europe. The idea that the ability to make war inhered in the blood of some populations more than in others was thus allowed to be expressed in the language of scientific 'fact'. However, the popularity of the theory had just as much to do with imperial imperatives post-1857.

Before the 1857 revolt, the high-caste Hindus of northern India were considered to be the most desirable recruits for the Bengal Army, which was central to the events that unfolded during the Mutiny. Yet, because they had played a central role in fermenting the rebellion in the Bengal Army they were soon cast as treacherous, faithless, deluded and easily incited to passion. Under the guise of the martial races theory these characteristics were cast as antithetical to the contemporary conceptions of manliness and this slowly legitimized the exclusion of these groups from the army. Those groups that had helped in quelling the rebellion – the Sikhs and Gurkhas in particular – became strongly associated with notions of fierce, gallant, honourable, loyal and courageous masculinity. They therefore became the best possible recruits.

The martial races theory led to policies that radically shifted the recruiting base of the Indian Army from Bengal and lower India to Punjab, Nepal and the western border areas of the Empire. In 1893 almost 44 per cent of the Indian Army was recruited from populations thought to produce martial races. By 1904 that number had risen to 57 per cent and by 1914 three-quarters of the native infantry was composed of martial races. This fetishisation of martiality is demonstrated by the contribution of Punjab, home to the most feted martial types – the Punjabi Muslims and the Sikhs – to the army. At the start of the war Punjab alone supplied almost half of the Indian Army's soldiery. During the war Sikhs comprised about 12.5 per cent of India's troops despite being only one per cent of the population. Only after more than two years of fighting did the need for men cause a loosening of the restrictions the British imposed on recruitment.

Sketches of soldiers in the Indian Army illustrate the narrow selection criteria of the British. The Gurkhas, Sikhs, Punjabi Muslims, and Pathans were among those that were widely considered martial races. The Pathan, while martial, was seen to have a weakness due to his volatile temperament.

W.F.
AN INDIAN REVERSE
FOR THE KAISER.

AN INDIAN REVERSE
FOR THE KAISER.

of *vilayat*? Were there encounters with European women and what was made of the different social mores? What was the first experience of the battlefield like? What were the stories, fears and worries the soldiers and their families shared with each other? And what impact did the war years and the experience have on the political and social milieu in India itself? These are important questions which research is only now and still very slowly beginning to give us answers to. And yet these are important questions to look at if we are to move beyond looking at Indian history just through the lens of simply the actions of elite politicians.

There were a number of factors motivating people to join the Indian Army. The most basic was, of course, economic benefit. The Indian Army in peacetime was an all-volunteer force taking in about 15,000 to 20,000 troops a year.[29] The men were a mixture of those who had been driven from the land, and migrant labourers happy to take advantage of the economic opportunities created by the colonial encounter. The pay for a sepoy in the run-up to the war was about Rs.11 a month (roughly equivalent Rs.14,000 a month in today's terms).[30] This amount was increased during active service to Rs.18 a month during the war (about Rs.25,800 today). In addition, sepoys also received a Rs.5 war *bhatta*, a Rs.50 bonus (roughly Rs.5,700 and Rs.57,000 in today's terms respectively) on enlistment and free rations in and out of active service. As the war progressed, the Indian Army also decided to allocate fertile plots of land to decorated sepoys.[31] Needless to say, these were all enormously welcome for a family that might have had few other sources of income.

In addition to financial incentives, some communities were attracted to the army by the martial self-image of their community. In some instances this self-image itself had been impacted by the British policy of recruiting only from certain areas (Punjab, the North-West Frontier Province, the United Provinces, and the kingdom of Nepal) and 'races' (Gurkhas, Punjabi Sikhs, Punjabi Muslims, Pathans, Dogras, Rajputs) of the subcontinent. Unsurprisingly those communities who were heavily recruited regarded themselves as the military elite and viewed their service to the *Sirkar* (government) as a way to maintain their status.[32] The words of the *Khalsa Advocate* in an

Previous pages (28-29): An invertible postcard celebrates German setbacks at the hands of Indian troops.
Above:A poster depicting Indians and Britons as brothers-in-arms marching to take on the German threat.

article published soon after the start of the war are telling in this respect:

> The Sikhs are a fighting nation and the first duty that is inculcated among them is duty of sacrifice. They are hardy, robust, bold and courageous. For instance, a Sikh when asked by somebody whether he would fight, replied he knew nothing else. To fight for those under whose protection they live is the sole business of the Sikhs, and really they know nothing else.[33]

Once in the army, soldiers showed a principled commitment to duty and *namak halali* (loyalty to one's superiors) even if this sense of duty could often be quite abstract. Some felt loyalty to God, others to their family. Yet others felt a personal duty to the King-Emperor himself. For some, the *Sirkar* was seen as the father to whom the soldiers had filial obligations. This relationship was often expressed in terms of having 'eaten the salt' of the government, a burden that could be repaid by performing one's duty.[34] Often loyalties to King, country, and God combined as can be seen from a letter written by an unknown writer in Punjab to a Sikh Jemadar who was serving in France with the 34th Sikh Pioneers:

> Keep your thoughts fixed on the Almighty and show your loyalty to the Government and to King George V. It is every man's duty to fulfil his obligations towards God, by rendering the dues of loyalty to his King. If in rendering the dues of loyalty he must yield his life, let him be ready to make even that sacrifice. Those heroes who have added lustre to the service of their country and their King, let them offer this prayer before God, that victory may be the portion of their King, and let them show the whole world how brave the people of India can be. The final prayer of this humble one before God Almighty is this – that God may make bright the heroes of Hindustan in the eyes of the world and with his healing hand soften the sufferings of the wounded to restore them to health, so that they may go back to the field of battle and render the dues of loyalty to their King of peace, King of kings, George V, and secure victory for him.[35]

Closely tied to this sense of duty was also the notion of *izzat* – concerns about shame, honour and masculinity.[36] Indian soldiers fought to gain or preserve their honour, standing, or reputation. The desire to win medals, to become a martyr or even negatively to ensure that they did not bring disrepute to their families or regiments were all

A recruitment poster from the war years entices Indians to join the army with promises of 'a lot of *izzat*' and 'very little danger'.

منی‌پور ریاست کے مزدوروں کی پلٹن اتحادیوں کو مغربی میدان میں مدد دی رہی ہے -
ਮਨੀਪੁਰ ਰਿਆਸਤ ਦੇ ਕੁਲੀਆਂ ਦੀ ਪਲਟਨ ਅੰਗਰੇਜ਼ਾਂ ਨੂ ਪਛਮੀ ਮੈਦਾਨ ਵਿਚ ਮਦਦ ਦੇ ਰੇਹੀ ਹੈ.
मणिपुरी मजदूरों के सैनिक दल के बागे जो पश्चिमप्रांत में सम्मिलित मित्रराज्यों की सेनाओं में नियुक्त हैं.
MEN OF THE MANIPURI LABOUR BATTALION WHO ARE EMPLOYED BY THE ALLIES ON THE WESTERN FRONT.

پلٹن کے قصاب پکانے کے لئے گوشت تیار کر رہے ہیں -
ਪਲਟਨ ਦੇ ਕਸਾਈ ਪਕਾਉਣ ਲਈ ਮਾਸ ਤਿਆਰ ਕਰ ਰੇਹੇ ਹਨ.
इस दल के कसाई लोग गोश्त पकाने के लिये तैयार कर रहे हैं.
THE BUTCHERS OF THE CORPS PREPARING CARCASES FOR A MEAL.

صابن اور چرٹ جنکے منی‌پوروالے بہت شایق ہیں دیئے جا رہے ہیں -
ਸਬੂਲ ਅਤੇ ਚੁਰਟ ਦਿਤੇ ਜਾ ਰੇਹੇ ਹਨ. ਮਨੀਪੁਰੀਏ ਇਹਨਾਂ ਚੀਜ਼ਾਂ ਦੇ ਅਧਕ ਪਿਆਰੇ ਹਨ.
आदमियों को साबुन और सिगारेट बांट देना। ये इन सब को बहुतही पसन्द करते हैं.
SOAP AND CIGARETTE RATIONS, WHICH THEY GREATLY APPRECIATE, BEING ISSUED TO THE MEN.

کلی کھانا کھا رہے ہیں - اِن کو رسد بہت فیاضی سے دی جاتی ہے -
ਮਜਦੂਰ ਖਾਣਾ ਖਾ ਰੇਹੇ ਹਨ. ਇਹਨਾਂ ਨੂ ਰਸਤ ਖੁਲੇ ਹਥ ਨਾਲ ਦਿਤੀ ਜਾਂਦੀ ਹੈ.
इस दल के आदमी खाना खा रहे हैं। उनको यथेष्ट परिमाण आहार मिलता है.
MEN OF THE CORPS ENGAGED IN A MEAL. THEY HAVE A VERY LIBERAL FOOD ALLOWANCE.

مزدور موٹرگاڑی کی بھال چال کر رہے ہیں - ایسی گاڑیاں اِنکو بہت حیران کر دیتیں ہیں -
ਕੁਲੀ ਮੋਟਰ ਗਡੀ ਨੂ ਵੇਖ ਰੇਹੇ ਹਨ. ਇਹਨਾਂ ਨੂ ਇਹੋ ਜੇਹੀਆਂ ਗਡੀਆਂ ਬਹੁਤ ਅਸਚਰਜ ਮਲੂਮ ਹੁੰਦੀਆਂ ਹਨ.
इस दल के आदमी बड़े शौक से एक मोटर-गाड़ी देख रहे हैं.
MEN OF THE CORPS EXAMINING A MOTOR-CAR, WHICH GREATLY EXCITES THEIR INTEREST.

مزدوروں کے خط و خال اور اُنکے قد کا اندازہ اِس تصویر سے بخوبی معلوم ہوتا ہے -
ਏਹ ਤਸਵੀਰ ਮਜਦੂਰਾਂ ਦੇ ਕਦ ਅਤੇ ਸ਼ਕਲ ਦਾ ਹਾਲ ਚਾਲ ਚੰਗੀ ਤਰਾਂ ਨਾਲ ਦਸਦੀ ਹੈ.
भिन्न भिन्न नमूने के आदमी जो इस दल में नियुक्त हैं.
VARIOUS TYPES OF MEN .WHO ARE EMPLOYED IN THE CORPS.

important motivations for soldiers to perform on the battlefield. The British themselves were not unaware of these numerous motivations. A Sikh soldier's letter from the 47th Sikhs brings this to life:

> Chur Singh has suffered martyrdom in the war. The 47th Sikhs were charging – Sahib said, "Chur Singh you are not a Sikh of Guru Gobind Singh, who sits in fear inside the trench!" Chur Singh was very angry. He gave order to his company to charge. He drew his sword and went forward.[37]

If the motivations of the soldiers seem strangely anachronistic, perhaps one reason was that conceptions of nationalism were different at the time. This is not to suggest that the soldiers were politically unaware or uncurious. Many showed a keen interest in following political developments at home. Others made keen observations about the alien countries they found themselves fighting in, tried to engage with these new cultures and drew comparisons with home.[38]

As the war progressed, the experience of the soldiers on the frontlines, in the trenches and in foreign countries challenged and changed the ways in which they approached colonial authority. Issues arose that began affecting morale. Soldiers chafed at their being sent back to the trenches soon after having recovered from injuries. 'We are all to be killed. Not a scrap of India is to be left', wrote Juvar Singh of the Bhopal Infantry while recovering in hospital in England.[39] Some were unhappy about the poor conditions of service, the inequality of pay and lack of opportunity for promotions.[40]

These factors occasionally led to tangible acts of dissent amongst Indian soldiers. Most commonly, soldiers wrote letters to their friends and family seeking to dissuade them from enlisting in the army. In May 1915, Havildar Abdul Rahman wrote to a friend to say:

> For God's sake don't come, don't come, don't come to War in Europe... and tell my brother Mohammed Yakub Khan for God's sake do not enlist. If you have any relatives, my advice is don't let them enlist. It is unnecessary to write any more.[41]

In more serious circumstances, they self-mutilated, deserted, and mutinied. By as early as late 1914, the British authorities started worrying about incidents of what they suspected were self-inflicted hand wounds which they dealt with in the harshest terms – execution for cowardice – to ensure that such cases stopped.[42] In some cases, soldiers were willing to risk the wrath of the military by defecting to the enemy or giving voice to their resentments at being made to fight their co-religionist Turks.

These cases of dissent and distress are minor anecdotes amongst the larger story of the overwhelming loyalty of the Indian Army during the four years of the war. But they do point to the ways in which Indian soldiers confronted with life outside India might have begun questioning how life carried on within it. As the subsequent chapters aim to show, the war made its Indian participants reflect on a diverse range of topics such as customs, manners, sensibilities, culture, education, hierarchy, the status of women, marriage, as well as the economic and physical environments that they became exposed to. These experiences, which no doubt had a lasting impact on the lives of those who lived through them and indeed impacted Indian politics in the immediate aftermath of the war, have failed to acquire any wider social recognition in India's historical consciousness.[43]

Facing page: A set of images show the men of a Manipuri labour battalion on the Western Front. The need for manpower during the war not only widened the recruitment base of the army beyond the traditional martial races, but also led to the government reaching out into previously untapped tribal and rural areas for much-needed labour.

As critical as understanding and acknowledging India's role and Indians' experiences in the war is, it is also a challenging endeavour. Mostly recruited from peasant backgrounds, the majority of Indian soldiers were not part of a tradition that would leave behind contemplative war memoirs. Stories of the war occasionally still survive in oral traditions, especially in heavily recruited regions of the country, but India's warriors largely took their reflections of their war experiences with them to their graves. This is not to say that the Indians did not contemplate or engage with the situations in which they found themselves. For example, from the start of the war the Indian Army encouraged its soldiers to write home once a week to assuage feelings of anxiety, despondency, and homesickness. By autumn 1915, Indian soldiers in France alone were exchanging nearly 50,000 letters.[44] More letters were sent home from soldiers on other fronts and no doubt ensured that the war was not as far away from the Indian imagination as we perhaps imagine today.

Some of these ruminations by Indians who took part in the war survive in disjointed fragments across the world. In colonial and imperial archives and personal collections, photographs, objects and even sound recordings from the war help bring alive, with gravity, sadness, and even humour, the strangeness of the Indian war experience. Some of these materials come with their own unique challenges. The most voluminous archive that relates the story of Indian soldiers who fought in the war, for example, survives in the form of censored letters written to and from Indians serving on the Western Front.[45] These bring their own challenges of interpretation having been often written by regimental scribes, read out openly and authored in awareness of military censorship.[46] War-time images often had their own propagandistic aims. Further, there are some war experiences we know much more about than others. The experience of the Indian soldier on the Western Front is perhaps best documented. Less material is available on the theatres of the Middle East and this holds even more true of the African campaigns, which makes telling a holistic story of the Indian war experiences a difficult prospect. As a result, this book does not claim to be a comprehensive guide to the Indian war experience. Rather, it hopes to bring together the current scholarship on India and the war, explore a few aspects of the Indian war experience through images, letters, memoirs and recordings of Indian troops and bring these to an audience that might not have been aware of this chapter in India's history.

During the war a wounded Sikh soldier wrote to his father from hospital asking rhetorically '... if I die here, who will remember me?'[47] The words reflect both the monstrous and the impersonal scale of the war and its isolating distance from everything the Indian soldier knew. Read today, they point at the amnesia about the war experience that affects historical memory in India. The words poignantly ask us, a century later, to revisit and understand the experiences and sacrifices of the Indian soldiers, many of whom died so far from home in the war of 1914-1918.

+++

Between August 1914 and November 1918, a total of 6,57,737 Indians were recruited to fight the Great War.

Muslims **198,969,** Rajputs **62,190,** Marathas **20,156,** Sikhs **88,925,** Gurkhas **55,589,** Jats **40,272,** Other Hindus **38,546,** Pathans **27,857,** Dogras **23,491,** Brahmans **20,382,** Ahirs **19,544,** Gujjars **18,296,** Tamils **16,390,** Rajputana Jats **14,967,** Burmese **12,163**

India's Economic Contribution to the War

India's contribution to the war effort was not simply limited to the supply of manpower. The burden of the war was also taken on in economic measure, both in terms of monetary assistance and in the form of materials. Such was the enthusiasm to contribute to the war effort in every manner that Indian members of the Imperial Legislative Council – the legislature of British India – unanimously urged the government 'to take into consideration the wish of the people of India to share in the heavy financial burden imposed upon the United Kingdom by the war.'

Monetary Assistance

Legally, India did not have to bear the cost of any military operations carried out beyond her own external frontiers. However, the Government of India decided that India would continue to pay the pre-war cost of maintenance of her troops sent overseas while the extra expenditure was met by Britain (i.e. India took on the burden that she would have had to shoulder had the forces remained stationed in India). For the period of the war this amounted to £29.6 million pounds (approximately £628 million pounds in current value). The Indian taxpayer paid not only for the remuneration (including free rations, gratuity, bonuses, and accommodation) of the Indian troops, but also for military measures taken to protect the North-West Frontier of the country (a worrisome border in even peaceful times that only acquired strategic importance during war time) and the country's coasts and ports. Additional costs also had to be borne for the employment of censors and the internment of hostile aliens and Prisoners of War.

At the beginning of 1917, the Government of India also offered the Imperial Government a lump sum of £100 million (in excess of £8 billion at current value) as a special contribution by India towards the expenses of the war. The amount was large enough to add 30 per cent to India's national debt and was at that time more than the country's annual income for an entire year. Prime Minister Lloyd George noted: 'Coming in addition to the enthusiasm and loyalty manifested throughout India at the outbreak of war and to the invaluable services since rendered by the Indian Army, this gift is to us a living proof that India shares wholeheartedly with the other subjects of the Crown in the ideals for which we are fighting in this war. That India should come forward of her own accord in this crisis and render such real and opportune assistance is not only a source of sincere satisfaction to His Majesty's Government, but must produce a better mutual understanding among all resources and people under the British Crown.'

Posters urged Indians to partake in the war economically by lending gold, such as the English poster (right), and by purchasing war bonds and certificates, as the posters in Bengali (p.36) and Gujrati (p.37) urged. Others emphasized the economic benefit of enrolling in the army. The Tamil poster (p.37) emphasizes a reward of Rs. 50 on enrolling, a Rs. 15 bonus and a Rs. 24 salary a month thereafter.

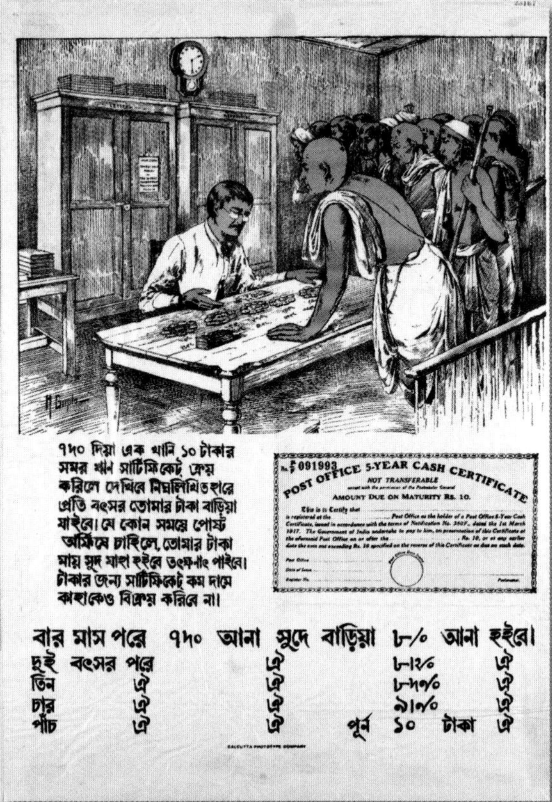

Material Assistance

In addition to these direct costs of the war, India also turned out to be an important repository of material assistance for the Allied war effort. Along with the troops, India sent 70 million rounds of ammunition, 60,000 rifles, and 550 guns to the main theatres of war. India also supplied enormous quantities of tents, boots, clothing, and saddlery. Later in the war, all the Indian planes and personnel of the Indian Air Force were at the disposal of the British.

As trench warfare set in on the Western Front, there was huge demand for sandbags. By July 1915, nearly 600,000 sandbags were needed per day for trench warfare. India was a priceless economic resource on this front as Britain's only supplier of jute. The Government of India reached agreements with Calcutta jute mills to supply sandbags for the army at a price below the market rate, along with 60 – 80,000 tons of raw jute per year that was sent to Dundee, which had jute-processing facilities, at cost price. India was also crucial in helping keep the soldiers properly booted by supplying cowhides for the purpose. During the war India provided enough leather to help prepare some 12 million pairs of army boots – sufficient for the whole British army and parts of the Russian and Italian armies.

The need to control the production of the economy to assist the war efforts became amply clear to the government as the war continued. The Defence of India Act 1915 gave the government the right to regulate, relocate, confiscate, and destroy private property – industrial enterprises, factories, workshops, mines, and land – in order to facilitate the war effort. The export of munitions and material needed to produce these as well as cattle, horses, mules, sheep, goats, hides, lead, and surgery stores were swiftly forbidden. A general ban on trade with Germany which, till the start of the war, was India's second largest trading partner was introduced. Restrictions were imposed on the 'export of foodstuffs and articles capable of being turned to warlike uses'. When hostilities broke out India became Britain's sole source of manganese ore and saltpetre, both of which were crucial for the manufacture of munitions and were completely diverted towards the war effort. Coal was requisitioned and was distributed by the Coal Controller. Wheat purchases had been placed under state control by early 1915. By the end of 1916, a Jute Control Scheme was under consideration and the export of all steel goods had been prohibited.

The war years and the economic constraints they imposed caused widespread distress to a majority of Indians, especially as a result of a steep leap in prices. For example, wholesale food prices in 1917 were 31 per cent above their pre-war levels. The rise in the prices of imported goods was even worse.

The one section of society that did benefit from the war were the business groups who kept trade

and industry going. In 1916-17 exports increased 21 per cent over the previous year and as Indian industry expanded to meet the war effort, the share of manufactured goods in India's exports jumped from less than 24 per cent in 1913-14 to 31 per cent in 1917-18. Interestingly, even the success of the Tata group, one of the largest conglomerates in India today, can be traced back to the effects of the First World War. The Tata Iron and Steel Company was the only steel producer in the British Empire east of the Suez and therefore vital to the Empire's war effort as hostilities spread beyond Europe. By September 1917, Tata was selling 78 per cent of its steel output to the government. In 1918 this amount rose to 98 per cent. During the war, the company supplied the government with 1,500 miles of rails and 300,000 tons of steel – materials that were essential for the campaigns in Mesopotamia, Egypt, Salonika, and East Africa, as well as for the Indian railways and military and civil departments of government.

These examples of monetary and material assistance were just some of the ways in which India's economic resources helped the war effort. It is not surprising that the Viceroy of the time, Lord Hardinge, had even as early as late 1914 noted that India had already 'been bled white by the War Office'.

The chargers of a cavalry division are pictured on the march in Crécy, France. Indian troops were dispatched to France soon after the outbreak of the war and played a crucial role in reinforcing the Allied position on the Western Front in the immediate months after their arrival.

France and Flanders

Fighting on the Western Front

Officers, Non Commissioned Officers and Men: I look to all my Indian soldiers to uphold the Izzat *of the British Raj against the aggressive and relentless enemy. I know with what readiness my loyal and brave Indian soldiers are prepared to fulfil this sacred trust on the field of battle, shoulder to shoulder with their comrades from all parts of the Empire. Rest assured that you will always be in my thoughts and prayers. I bid you go forward to add fresh lustre to the glorious achievements and noble traditions, courage and chivalry of my Indian Army, whose honour and fame are in your hands.*

MESSAGE FROM KING GEORGE V
TO INDIAN TROOPS DEPARTING FOR THE WESTERN FRONT[1]

+++

God knows whether the land of France is stained with sin or whether the Day of Judgement has begun in France. For guns and of [sic] rifles there is now a deluge, bodies upon bodies, and blood flowing. God preserve us, what has come to pass! From dawn to dark and from dark to dawn it goes on... our guns have filled the German trenches with the dead and made them brim with blood. God grant us grace, for grace is needed. Oh God, we repent! Oh God, we repent!

AMIR KHAN (129TH BALUCHIS)
TO LANCE NAIK KHAN ZAMAN (RAWALPINDI DISTRICT, PUNJAB)[2]

+++

In eastern France, near the village of Neuve Chapelle, amidst open fields and the occasional traffic stands a sanctuary enclosed by a circular wall with intricate *jali* work and carvings. A 15-feet high column surmounted with a lotus capital, the Imperial British Crown and the Star of India dominates the foreground. On either side of the column are two tigers, silently observing those passing by and guarding the site. The column itself is engraved with the phrase 'God is One, He is the Victory' in languages foreign to the country – English, Hindi, Urdu, and Gurmukhi. The base of the column bears the inscription 'India 1914–1918'.[3]

The memorial is strikingly incongruous in rural France but it is a fitting location to commemorate over 4,700 Indian soldiers and labourers who lost their lives on the Western Front. Neuve Chapelle was where the Indian Corps fought its first action as a single unit. At the Battle of Neuve Chapelle (10–13 March 1915) the Indian infantry formed half the attacking force and it was in the fierce fighting here that the Indian Corps lost about 20 per cent of its strength. Designed by Sir Herbert Baker, who along with Sir Edwin Lutyens conceptualized imperial New Delhi, the memorial takes its inspiration from the Ashokan Sanchi stupa. The peaceful fields that surround the memorial today almost belie the bitter violence the Indian troops who fought here had to face. It was here that piles of their wriggling, writhing bodies lay on the ground, and the air resounded with shrieks, groans and curses. It was this site that witnessed tragic scenes of the wounded attempting to shelter themselves behind parapets formed of bodies of their comrades, while others dug their own graves.[4]

When the war broke out in 1914, the involvement of the Indian Army in the conflict in Europe was not a given. The Indian Army's primary concerns were the defence of India itself and the protection of British interests in India's immediate neighbourhood. The possibility of sending troops abroad was a secondary consideration and yet the need for trained men to stem the German advance on the Western Front became so immediate that India's army was quickly identified as a crucial source of manpower for the war effort.[5] India responded to the call for men by immediately mobilising an expeditionary force of two infantry divisions and one cavalry brigade – Expeditionary Force 'A' – that was to find itself in the thick of the conflict on the Western Front a mere month after the war had broken out.

By October 1914, the Indian troops were already involved in some of the heaviest fighting on the Western Front and they continued to play a central role on the front till December 1915, when the infantry was withdrawn due to sagging morale and the bitter winter and sent to Mesopotamia with just a lone cavalry division left in France. During this time, 89,335 sepoys and 49,273 Indian labourers were involved in some of the key battles of the Western Front, including Ypres, Givenchy, Neuve Chapelle, Second Ypres, Festubert, and Loos.

A warm welcome

In the heat of late August and early September the Lahore and Meerut Divisions and the Secunderabad Cavalry Brigade gathered in Karachi and Bombay. India's involvement in the war had been confirmed and the authorities scrambled to mobilize rations and fodder for the troops and round up ships that could be amended for military use and to carry men and animals to the site of battle. Even though the final destination was not known, winter clothing was gathered.[6] For the troops, this was already turning out to be a great adventure. As they waited for their departure, they were kept busy with sight-seeing tours of the cities that had been organized by their regiments. When not busy being tourists, infantry regiments went on marches around the city and into the neighbouring countryside while the cavalry groomed and exercised their horses.[7] The overall morale among the troops was buoyant. Worried that the war might be over before they even got involved, they were keen to be in the thick of fighting at the earliest.

On 22 August 1914, the first troops from India set sail to join the war.[8] Over the next few weeks more troops would join them in making their way to the battlefront. For most soldiers this was their first journey across the *kala pani*. Individual regiments had prepared for cleansing ceremonies on the troops' return but there was still nervousness about setting sail on the vast expanse of water that stretched into the horizon. 'Truly, the black, or rather blue, water seemed uncanny, spreading for thousands of miles,' thinks Lalu, the protagonist of Mulk Raj Anand's *Across the Black*

Waters, which is a rare literary telling of Indian soldiers' experiences of the First World War. 'It seemed as if God had spat upon the universe and the spittle had become the sea. The white flecks of the foam on the swell, where wave met wave, seemed like the froth churned out of God's angry mouth.'[9]

A few weeks later, on 26 September 1914, the Lahore Division became the first fully formed body of Indian troops to disembark at Marseilles. The reception the troops received was ecstatic. It was a glorious autumn day and as the troops marched through the streets of the town, a curious and welcoming crowd of mostly women and children greeted them with chants of '*Vivent les hindous*'. Photographs from the time show the 15th Sikhs marching through the streets, proud and upright, greeted by a populace throwing flowers to celebrate the new arrivals to the heart of the battle. The commotion and excitement of the scene were infectious. 'Any fool can see they are greeting us with warmth and hospitality,' says a sepoy in *Across the Black Waters* as he urges his fellow soldiers to respond with cries of 'Long live the *Francisis!*'

This initial excitement at being in a foreign land and at this enthusiastic welcome ebbed quickly. The Indian troops arriving in France were immediately diverted to fill in the gaps left by the heavy losses suffered by the British Expeditionary Force. The Indian troops had arrived in France at a critical moment in the early months of the war, when the British corps in Flanders was exhausted, demoralized and without reserves. The pressing need for reinforcements meant that Indian battalions were fed piecemeal as attachments to British divisions. Even as the Indian soldiers provided reinforcement on the frontlines the wet, cold weather, the heavy casualties and brutality of modern warfare quickly began taking a heavy toll on the morale of the soldiers. Despite this, the additional manpower that the Indian troops provided was crucial for the Allied war effort in what had already become a painstakingly slow war of attrition.[10]

A difficult war

A persistent problem for the Indian troops during their stay in France and Flanders was the unfamiliar weather and their being woefully ill-equipped to face it. In some ways, the early months of the war saw Indian troops fighting two enemies – the Germans and the cold. It was already autumn by the time the Indians reached France and a cold winter was imminent. By November itself, night-time temperatures in the trenches were falling to -10°C with heavy rain, frost, and snow.[11] An Indian soldier, Gulab Singh, wrote home saying: 'Many men have had their feet cut off for they had been burnt by the frost.'[12] While the Indian Corps had left India with winter clothing, these were suitable for the milder, sunnier winters of the Indian plains, not the biting and freezing cold of Europe, and definitely not the winter of 1914, which was recorded as one of the coldest in memory. The uniforms provided to the troops were of khaki drill, a thin cotton cloth that was totally inadequate for the rain, wind, sleet and snow of the French winter. The thicker khaki serge uniforms would not be available for the Indians till December; some units such as the Sirhind Brigade of the Lahore Division did not receive winter clothing until early 1915.[13]

While attempts were made to issue some provisional warm clothing to the Indians in the meantime, even this exercise in improvising uniforms was not without its challenges. One of the first tasks given to the interpreter of the 1/9th Gurkha Rifles, for example, was to go to the market and purchase 3,000 safety pins so that the men could adjust the long johns given to them to size. Even though each man was supposed to have been issued with an extra blanket on arrival, there was a shortage of these and Indian soldiers were for a while found wrapped in eiderdowns, tablecloths and even cast-off curtains to ward of the cold.[14]

The inhospitable weather was relentless for the Indian troops and they often developed a sense of humour as a coping mechanism. In a letter Nattha Singh, a signaller with the 2nd Lancers tried to explain to a Dafadar friend with the 7th Lancers in Mesopotamia the difficulties the weather posed:

> The cold here is excessive. Here are two stories about it. One day, three or four of us signallers were working at the telegraph and telephone. When the message we were at was finished, a Jat added through the wire 'if this cold continues for a month of two we shall leave the earth with pleasure'. When I think of this story, or hear it told as a joke, I laugh out loud. The second story is that on the 19th of November I began writing a letter and found that the ink was frozen in the inkstand. I broke the ink-pot, took out the ink, melted it over a fire, and wrote the letter to you with the melted ink.[15]

The Indian Soldiers' Fund, a charity set up in London in October 1914 to provide material comforts to Indian troops on the Western Front, played an important role in providing much needed garments (and much else) for the troops. Yet warm clothing was only one factor that alleviated the difficult conditions. Even when the winter ended, spring offered little respite to the men. The men had to stay huddled in the trenches, brave the gusts of rain and wind, survive the flooded trenches and fight in the wet and muddy landscape. A Garwahli soldier wrote to his father:

> It is very hard to endure the bombs, father. It will be difficult for anyone to survive and come back safe and sound from the war...The bullets and cannon-balls come down like snow. The mud is up to a man's middle.[16]

The conflation of snow with bullets and cannon-balls in their potential for devastation in the soldier's mind is telling.

Trench foot, caused by reduced circulation in the feet and legs due to continuous standing in cold water and mud, quickly became a serious issue for a number of units.[17] When ordered into the firing line at the end of 1914 the condition of the men of the Poona Horse was so bad that it took the unit one and a half hours to walk one and a half miles.[18] Men of the 2/8th Gurkhas began marching barefoot because it was less painful that marching with their boots on.[19]

As challenging as acclimatising to the weather was, it was not as difficult as becoming used to the peculiar nature of this war. Indians troops had largely seen duty manning the Indo-Afghan border, battling tribesmen or putting down local resistance in the Northwest Frontier Province or elsewhere in the Empire.[20] This was very different from the kind of war they were expected to fight on the Western Front.

Many soldiers were not even properly prepared for trenches where they had to spend a large part of the war. These snaking networks of subterranean tunnels with barbed wires, bunkers, saps and machine gun nests were bizarre and unexpected. Viewing the battlefield trenches for the first time Lalu in *Across the Black Waters* wonders, 'But why were these trenches so shapeless and irregular?

They were so different from the regular trenches built for mimic warfare in the parade grounds at Ferozepur.'[21] As the soldiers descend into the slimy, pockmark network of trenches in the novel, 'a hail of lead' greets them. 'The sepoys tried to keep their backs bent and heads lifted', as they had been told to do. All around, groups of British soldiers stood in the trenches behind sandbags, firing the occasional shot with their rifles at an unseen enemy. Somewhere in the distance heavy artillery belches, one after the other, 'but neither the earth, nor the sky, nor the air seemed to be any different after the thunder had died down' as if the guns were booming in 'some unknown world, far away.'[22] This was the life the sepoys had to immediately adapt to. The tedious and ponderous nature of the war comes through in Havildar Abdul Rahman's words, 'For six months I have not taken off my boots for one second, nor taken off my uniform, nor have I had one good night's rest.'[23]

If the trenches in their chaos were a shock to the soldiers, one can only imagine their reaction to the kinds of mechanised ammunition being used or to the chemical gas warfare that took place during the war. Daya Ram of the 2nd Lancers wrote home to Ambala, Punjab explaining the war:

> The fighting is very severe. The moves are like those of a game of chess. When an attack is made in one direction a countermove is made in another, and attention is drawn off the first attack. The war is on entirely new lines and is full of surprises. It is impossible to understand it. At present we are in the trenches waiting for orders. We do not know what will happen. A new kind of smoke [gas?] has been invented which is let loose in the trenches and if you get a sniff of it you lose consciousness at once. It does not matter whether you are armed or not, as you lose all your senses. Such inventions have been made that one's mind is utterly confused. There is a new kind of gas that catches fire directly it is let out the cylinder. It is liquid fire and burns anyone who is in front of it. It is real magic.[24]

Confronted with the need to prove his loyalty and bravery in the war, one soldier wrote home in frustration to try and convey just how different this war was from what he had expected:

> What you say in your letter about not being disloyal to the Emperor, and it being the religion of Sikhs to die facing the foe – all that you say is true. But only if you yourself could be here and see for yourself! Any shrivelled charas-sodden fellow can fire the gun and kill a score of us at our food in the kitchen. ... Wherever you look, machine guns and canon begin to shoot, and bombs fly out which kill every man they hit. The earth is mined and filled with powder; when men walk upon it, the powder is lit and up go the men! There is no fighting face to face. Guns massacre regiments sitting ten miles off. Put swords or pikes or staves in our hands..., then indeed we should show you how to fight face to face. But if no one faces us, what can we do?[25]

The destruction wreaked by this new kind of war was poignantly evoked by Santa Singh, who wrote to his mother:

> Many sons of mothers, brothers of sisters, and brothers of mothers have been lying dead for a whole year on the field of battle. A year has passed and there they lie. He who sees them for the first time says there is no place left empty. All the ground is covered with corpses. So many corpses are there, and all have perished in forty seconds. As a man climbs a plum tree and shakes down the plums [so that] they fall and lie in heaps, so are men here fallen ... They too are the children of mothers.[26]

To add to the devastation the soldiers witnessed, there was also a sense of incoherence as army units that had been decimated by the fighting were reconstituted piecemeal. Only furthering the sense of confusion was the Indian troops' dependence on their British officers to communicate and command. Unlike many other colonial armies, in the Indian Army it was the white officer who had to learn the native language rather than the other way round. By the end of 1914 the Indian battalions that had suffered heavy losses had only four or five white officers as opposed to the standard twelve.[27] As the casualties of white officers in the Indian units mounted, it no doubt affected the morale and effectiveness of Indian troops.[28]

It is not surprising then that in the first few weeks of combat more than half of the Indians admitted to hospital had sustained hand wounds that the British thought might have been self-inflicted.[29] Such an assessment was probably too harsh and more indicative of British fears of dropping morale. Clearly, though, such instances did indicate how desperately some Indian soldiers might have wanted to extricate themselves from the situation they were in. Unfortunately, there was no easy escape route. In an attempt to stem such occurrences, court-martials were convened, several men tried and some even shot for cowardice.[30] No doubt, the men quickly realized that in addition to risking extremely harsh punishments, unlike their previous experiences in India where an injury would excuse the soldier from further involvement in a campaign, this war would require them to return to the front as soon as they had recovered from any injuries.

Despite the challenges, many soldiers displayed astounding bravery and courage in the midst of war. Many were truly committed to the cause of a victory for the King and Empire, and considered it an honour and privilege to fight. Lance Dafadar Dip Chand of the 29th Lancers wrote to his friend:

> ... You must realize that this is the time for brave men. I have Government work to do, and I must do it heartily. I consider it an honour that I am called to do this work, and that I am looked upon as a loyal subject. Do not be anxious. If I do not see you again, my name will be written in letters of gold and inscribed in the list of brave. Then you will be proud of your friend who has given his life for the Sirkar. Our Government has done everything possible to make things easy for us and provided us with every comfort, but up to date I have not been able to make any recompense. Now is the time.[31]

Indian soldiers won a number of gallantry medals serving on the Western Front. Indians had become eligible to win the Victoria Cross (the highest military decoration awarded for valour in the face of the enemy by the British) in 1911 and the first award of the honour to an Indian was to Khudadad Khan in October 1914. In total, six of the eleven Victoria Crosses that Indian soldiers won during the war were for the bravery and courage they displayed while fighting in France and Flanders. A German soldier who had fought against Indian troops wrote to the *Frankfurt Zietung*, 'Today for the first time we had to fight the Indians. At first we spoke with contempt of the Indians. Today we learnt to look on them in a different light.'[32]

Contrasting cultures

For the Indian soldiers, the war was not just a military experience. It also afforded them a social education and opened up worlds, situations and relationships far removed from anything they would have been used to.

For many Indians, the war sharply highlighted the racist dimensions of colonial rule. For example, every time the Indian troops' morale plummeted or performance suffered, concerns were raised about the discipline and loyalty of the troops.[33] Thakur Amar Singh, who served as Aide-de-camp to the Sirhind Brigade perceptively picked up on and articulated this undercurrent when he wrote in his diary, 'the great trouble under which we have laboured is that whenever we fail in the slightest degree anywhere, people raise a hue and cry whereas if the British troops fail under the same circumstances no one mentions it. ... Plainly the thing is that if there is a success it is due to the British element but if there is a reverse then it is all down to the Indian troops. I do not know what is expected of the Indians.'[34]

Even when it became clear that systemic issues were hindering the performance of Indian troops, no effort was taken to address these. For example, replacing the British officers of the Indian units quickly became an issue, as it was difficult to find officers with knowledge of Indian languages and culture. Still, the British resisted granting King's Commissions to Indians that would allow Indians to become officers in the Army. Sir James Willcocks, Commander of the Indian Corps in France, for example, admitted that granting King's Commissions to Indians would be a wise move politically, but was adamant that Indians could not equal white officers. 'No one has a greater admiration for the Indian soldier, and officer when he lives up to it, than I have,' wrote Willcocks. 'He's generally brave, nearly always loyal – but he is seldom *if ever* fit to replace the British officer. Immediately you touch on this point you strike the bedrock of the reason we own India. The Indian is simply not fit to lead his men against Europeans; he will lead a charge or cover a retirement, but if he has to think, he fails. ... It is the presence and natural instincts of the white man which the Indian Officer can *never* replace. Indeed as I range over the whole field of possibilities, I cannot conceive of a case in which the Indian officer can be given the status and responsibility of a British officer... The Indian has not the instincts which make leaders in *modern* war. Of course I do not deny that amongst them there must be some such men, but after 37 years service I cannot put my hand on *one*... There is in fact no solution; the European and Indian are built on different lines, the one to command men, the other to wait for guidance before he issues his commands.'[35]

Despite having allowed Indians to fight in Europe, the colonial state's preeminent concern was the maintenance of racial superiorities. Denying Indians KCOs by arguing that only a white man could be a leader in war was a way to reinforce this belief. Instead, the war exposed many of the Indian troops to attitudes that made them question the racial hierarchies they had so far taken to be incontrovertible and indeed made them more willing to dissent and defy British orders. The self-inflicted wounds were only one example of this. In addition, Indian soldiers also observed the more relaxed social order of French colonialism. In *Across the Black Waters,* the soldiers come across '*habshis*' (the Hindi-Urdu word for a black person) and Moors who are soldiers of the French army. Lalu, the protagonist, notes, 'At Marseilles he had seen a few African soldiers talking openly to girls in the cafes and the French sahibs did not mind, though he himself had been surprised, for the English did not like even the brown-skinned Indians to look at white women. He wondered how the English liked the French being so free and easy. And if

Sex and Romance in France

In India relationships between white women and Indian men were generally frowned upon. Concerns about 'Western' women falling under the thrall of 'Eastern' men were endemic, stoked by images of lascivious sepoys raping and dismembering white women during the 1857 mutiny. It was strongly felt that the elite status of white women had to be carefully protected and that even consensual relations between Indian men and white women would undermine the colonial hierarchy.

Interracial interactions were easy to police in India. Social mores since the mid-1800s made British women in India limit their contact with Indians to a minimum and the severe penalties for pursuing a relationship with a white woman made it unlikely for Indian men to seek such relationships. Even when it came to the Indian army, the British were not unduly concerned with the morality of the Indian soldiers except when this concerned white women. The primary concern that motivated any attempt to limit sexual activity was the danger of venereal disease. Tellingly, when en route to fight in Europe during the war some Indian units disembarked in Egypt, few attempts were made to limit sexual contacts beyond reminding the men that catching a preventable venereal disease was a punishable offence. Once Indian soldiers were on the Western Front, however, British anxieties mounted. Most French men were away at the war and the French had few of the racial preoccupations of the British. As one British bureaucrat put it: 'the French allow their African troops the same privileges as Europeans: [he] is as good as a Frenchman, whereas the Indian is kept under various restrictions.' Clearly, the possibilities for sexual contact were plentiful and became enough of a source of concern that the authorities began to enforce strict controls on the off-base activities of Indian soldiers. Soldiers who stayed out after 11 pm were deemed to be 'seeking romance' and could be subject to a punishment of a dozen lashes, though this was rarely applied.

It was not just the British who were worried about these relationships, though. The sepoys themselves were worried about wayward wives and their marriages failing. 'All the men are away... all the women are rampant,' wrote one correspondent from the North-West Frontier to his friend serving in France. There were also concerns amongst the sepoys' families back home, particularly the women, about the temptations they faced. Soldiers often wrote to their families back home to reassure them that they would not get involved with foreign women:

> 'My father, I swear in the God and His Prophet and declare that there is no [ground for suspicion]. Am I such a wretch and such a blackguard as to leave my noble wife and child and behave thus?'

Still there were sepoys who did strike up relationships with French women and these often became points of conversation at the front and back home. 'I have heard about your amours with French women and how the officers forbid it,' wrote Farrior Major Khan from Punjab to Wali Mahomed Khan who was serving with the 18th Lancers in France. One Punjabi soldier wrote home to his friend telling him about his plans for his New Year's celebrations: 'In every village there are four or five hotels, and each of these today is an ample realization of the paradise of which we have read in books and heard from Mullahs... I send you a picture of a girl. When you see it, you will understand what beauty there is in France.' Such praise was not one-sided. When the troops moved on from Marseilles it was reported that some men had received letters that were of a 'violently amatory nature'. One woman wrote to an Indian soldier: 'At present the troops here are Irish but they have not the same sympathy with us as you used to show.'

While many of these relationships might have been transactional or fleeting, some did develop into longer-term attachments. As a result – and in a bid to maintain morale – from late 1916 the British and French authorities agreed that Muslim soldiers might be permitted to marry French women. (The circumscribed nature of this approval stemmed from the fact that a Muslim man could marry a Jewish or Christian woman if his bride converted to Islam and could therefore marry a Frenchwoman without losing his religion. A Hindu would risk losing caste by marrying out, something the British clearly did not want to be seen as encouraging.) However, fears of loss of religion persisted and cases of marriage were not without controversy. Such was the case when Mahomed Khan, a trooper in the 6th Cavalry, married a Frenchwoman. A fellow sepoy wrote:

> There was an extraordinary affair in the regiment yesterday, although there have been similar incidents before in other regiments. Mahomed Khan, the lance dafadar, is engaged to a Frenchwoman on the condition that he becomes a Christian. The marriage ceremony is to take place in two or three days. We have done our best to prevent it, but all has been in vain. You can judge the state of affairs when it has got to the length of our marrying Frenchwomen.

Mohamed Khan's family was so hostile to the union that he claimed he had been personally ordered by the King to marry the woman and that he would have got into 'grave trouble' had he refused.

We have no clear sense of how many men might have married French women or the extent of dalliance between French women and Indian soldiers, but we clearly know that such romantic interactions, even if few and far between, did take place and were talked about. They became, in a way, another means by which life in Europe was experienced by the Indian soldiers and perhaps even offered a contrast against which the more personal aspects of life and relationships in India could be measured.

This war-era postcard provides a hint at the attraction some Indian soldiers held for French ladies.

the French liked the blacks, why shouldn't he like them? Why had he thought himself superior? He felt ashamed.'[36]

If their experience in France made the soldiers question the racial hierarchies of colonial rule it also made them question the status quo in India itself and often acutely analyse why India was both underdeveloped and subjugated. Now that they had seen the West, comparisons were easy to make. Many soldiers made perceptive observations about the wealth they saw here and the role of education, religion, and women in society.[37] Soldiers were quick to notice the differences in everyday life, particularly in living standards and agricultural practices, which was perhaps not surprising given the agrarian background of most of the soldiers. This comes across starkly through the first questions that the soldiers have for a French man they meet in *Across the Black Waters*. 'Did you ask whether he owned land, whether they plough the land, like us, with oxen? Whether they use a plough to break the soil, and scythe and sickle to the cut the crop and flail? And how they thresh?' asks a character in the novel.[38] In real life, Saif Ali, a Pathan serving in France had similar agrarian concerns:

> The country is very fine, well watered and fertile. The fields are very large and full of trees. Every man's land yields him thousands of maunds of wheat ... If one were to plant a garden anywhere, it would grow.[39]

Their stay on the Western Front also gave soldiers the opportunity to observe the differences in social and cultural norms between the home and abroad. On occasion this sparked revelations about the need for education and even gender reform. Several men wrote home commenting on the fact that in France all children were obliged to attend school. Teja Singh of the 9th Hodson's Horse in France observed:

> The custom in this country is that when a child is five years old he is sent to school. ... These (the French) people appear to be superior to us solely because of education. Learning is a great benefit.[40]

Lance Dafadar Mahomed Khan wrote to home to Rawalpindi offering to pay for a teacher at the local mosque to school both boys and girls. 'In my young days I did not learn anything, and to this day I am regretting my mistake.'[41] Ranji Lal of Rohtak wrote to his grandfather:

> When I look at Europe I bewail the lot of India. In Europe everyone, man and woman, boys and girls are educated. The men are at war and the women are doing the work. They write to their husbands and get their answers. You ought to educate your girls and our posterity will be the better for it.[42]

As the soldiers' letters above show, the men's observations on education intersected with their observation about the French women, who offered a striking contrast to the womenfolk at home. Indian soldiers sometimes became romantically or sexually involved with women abroad, but some of the most poignant bonds they formed were with French matrons in whose homes they were billeted. Sowar Wali Mohammed Khan sent home a letter from his French 'mother', which said 'as long as [he] remains in this country [France] he shall, so far as it rests with me, want for nothing since he is dear to me as a son.' Wali Mohammed's mother replied thanking the Frenchwoman for the kindness and hospitality she had shown to her son and inviting her to come to India with him on his return.[43]

Another soldier wrote home explaining the bond he had built with the lady he was staying with:

> I have seen strange things in France. The French are a sympathetic and gracious people. Some time ago we were established for about three months in a village. The house in which I was billeted was the house of a well-to-do man, but the only occupant was the lady of the house and she was advanced in years. Her three sons had gone to war. One had been killed, another had been wounded and was in hospital and the third was at that time in the trenches. There is no doubt that the lady was very much attached to her sons. There are miles of difference between the women of India and the women of this country. During the whole three months I never once saw this old lady sitting idle although she belonged to a high family. Indeed during the whole three months she ministered me to such an extent that cannot adequately describe her kindness. Of her own free will she washed my clothes, arranged my bed, polished my boots for three months. She used to wash down my bedroom daily with warm water. Every morning she used to prepare and give me a tray with bread, butter, milk and coffee. I was continually wishing to find a way to reimburse her the expense; but however much I pressed she declined. When we had to leave the village the old lady wept on my shoulder. Strange that I had never seen her weeping for her dead son but she should weep for me![44]

The time they spent in France and Flanders was deeply impressed on the consciousness of the Indians who were serving on the Western Front. As one soldier wrote, 'Here our constitutions have become strangely changed.'[45] Here they had both come face-to-face with the brutality of war and experienced Europe and interacted with Europeans on a more equal footing than ever before. Some have claimed that this close encounter with Europe at large weakened imperial authority and contributed to crises that plagued the Empire between 1918 and 1922. Prominent historian Sir Percival Spear, for example, noted that 'village India saw Europe in its sordid wartime clothes and was not impressed.'[46] There might be some truth in this statement. Sitting in the trenches, facing German bombardment, Lalu in *Across the Black Waters* thinks, 'If he had been told even a fortnight ago that in *Vilayat,* the land of his dreams, where he had been so happy and eager to come as on an adventure, the sahibs, whom he admired so much, were wilfully destroying each other, ruining their villages and cities, he would not have believed it.'[47] For many soldiers, though, despite the horrors of war, the country they were serving in left numerous positive imprints for its wealth, education, relative egalitarianism and industry. It was no doubt an encounter that would make them view home very differently.

+++

The Indian Soldiers' Fund

As soon as it was announced that Indian soldiers would be involved in the war effort there was considerable interest in India and in Britain to help towards the relief of the sick and wounded and to contribute funds and gifts of food and clothing to the troops of the Indian army. Various appeals and much correspondence reached the India office on the subject. In particular, concerns were raised by former army officers who were worried about the Indian troops fighting in cold and harsh conditions that they were not used to.

A former Quarter Master General of the Indian Army wrote to the India Office to bring to its attention the challenges Indian soldiers might face fighting on the Western Front. The Indian troops were due to arrive in France at a time when autumn would already be well advanced and with a severe winter in prospect. In his letter to the government, the General suggested contributions for the Indian troops consisting of 'good warm socks', comforters to protect the upper parts of the soldiers' chest and back, short cardigans and warm gloves of soft wool in addition to cocoa, coffee, tea, and rum. These recommendations were based on his 'experiences in Afghanistan when men died in scores from pneumonia.'

Things had, of course, changed since the Anglo-Afghan war. For their service in France troops were supposed to be given a clothing supply that included a great-coat, socks, a jersey, a pair of mittens, warm pyjamas, a country blanket, a balaclava cap, a flannel shirt, a pair of warm drawers, and a warm vest. However, it was quickly realized that additional comforts would be welcome, both in the field and in hospitals. It was felt that these acts of charity would supplement official efforts since losses in clothing

Indian soldiers sort through their belongings at the military camp in Ashurst. Though Indian troops were provided for by the army, it was felt that official efforts could be supplemented by private acts of charity, and to coordinate which, the Indian Soldier Fund was set up in 1914.

INDIANS AT ASHURST.

and materials were bound to occur on the front. Furthermore, additional comforts in hospitals would doubtless improve the soldiers' morale.

To address this need the Indian Soldiers' Fund was formed under the control of the St. John Ambulance Association, a first aid charity, to collect and administer funds for the welfare of Indian troops. The administering committee of the Fund included, among others, Lord Curzon, the Agha Khan, Ratan Tata, and the Maharani of Bharatpur.

Among the first tasks the Fund took on was to draft a comprehensive list of articles acceptable as gifts for the use of Indian troops on active service, based on feedback from the men themselves. These offer an interesting insight in what the soldiers most valued, wanted and needed on the front. Only gifts that could be easily packed and would not deteriorate on their long voyage were considered. A list of items that could be sent to the front was agreed upon and included the following:

Warm socks (most acceptable of all gifts of clothing)	Cigarettes	Sweets of all sorts
Long woollen stockings	Matches (packed in tins)	Plain chocolate (in ¼ lb. packages)
Gloves, warm	Cheap electric hand lamps	Sugar (in 1 lb. parcels, in 50 lb. bags). {Very much appreciated; should be brown and as coarse as possible}
Gloves, without separate fingers, except forefinger	Tobacco	Maple sugar
Jerseys	Pipes (plain briar)	Tinned milk (sweetened preferred)
Woollen comforters	Folding candle lanterns	Curry powder
Knitted *puggaries*	A few hair clipping machines and razors (10 per regiment)	Spices – Cinnamon, cloves, cardamom, areca nut (in 10 lb. tins)
Warm vests	Notepaper	Figs
Balaclava caps (thin over ears)	Envelope	Raisins
Waterproof covers for *puggaries*	Night lights	Cocoa
Kumarbands, sewing kit, strong buttons, needles, cotton	Plain postcards	Salt
	Pencils	Tea

Over the course of the Indian troops' engagement in Europe, hundreds of kilos of condiments like spices, chutney, and curry powder and sweets like jiggery and *pinni* (a Punjabi sweet made from lentils) were shipped to the front. In 1915 some 62,000 tins of coconut oil were also provided to the soldiers who mostly used it to oil their hair. As the Indian troops moved to more war fronts, additional items suitable for the troops were added to the list. It was noted that sunglasses would be welcomed by troops serving in East Africa. The Fund was also sent ad-hoc gifts from dignitaries. In January 1915, for example, Sir James Willcocks noted that a 'most useful' gift of Vaseline had been sent to the troops by the Maharaja of Scindia. Other dignitaries, like the Begum of Bhopal and the Maharaja of Rewa, donated amounts of money that could be expended on comforts for Indian troops at the front at the discretion of Her Majesty's Government.

The Soldiers' Fund also quickly came to the conclusion that 'His religion is very close [to] the heart of the Oriental' and worked to provide religious texts and objects to keep up the morale of the troops. At one point the Fund received 900 copies of the Quran from the Begum of Bhopal and 300 copies of the Granth Sahib from donors in Punjab. Sets of the *Kara*, *Kirpan*, *Kangha*, *Khanda* and *Kachera* were made under the personal supervision of the son of the Prime Minister of Patiala before being sent to the front and the Maharani of Bhavnagar donated some 345 copies of the Bhagwad Gita and 3,350 rosaries.

The words of thanks from an Indian Labour Company in France made clear the impact the Fund's work had on the morale of the troops:

> On behalf of our men may I tender you our thanks for the gifts, especially for the kindliness of spirit which has prompted them, and which cheers our men to feel that there are, close by, kindly hearts feeling and thinking for them in this distant land.

A total of 85,953 Horses, 65,398 Ponies and Mules, 10,781 Camels, 5,061 Draught Bullocks and 5,622 Dairy Cattles were sent from India to the Great War 1914-18 to various fronts.

These figures include horses and mules obtained from abroad and shipped to the various theatres after being trained in India.

Above and facing page: The *SS Akbar*, pictured here, set sail from Bombay on 28 August 1914 for Marseille, packed to capacity with the men of the 47th Sikhs. The ship carried not just soldiers to the battlefront, but also horses and mules.

12
↑3088
3

Facing page and above: Indian troops gathered in Marseilles from where they continued their journey further north to French towns like Orleans, which were closer to the battlefront.

Above and facing page: Indian troops board trains taking them to the war front.

GUERRE de 1914
4 - Passage des Troupes Hindoues
Edit. du Courrier du Centre - Limoges
K1F 51887

Contingents of an Indian labour corps are pictured arriving in France. A number of Indians were shipped to the front in auxiliary roles – as followers, drivers, cooks and labourers, amongst other roles.

Troops receive their mail at the Post Office headquarters of the Indian Corps in Merville, France. In a bid to alleviate homesickness, the British encouraged Indian troops to write letters home. The Indians took this encouragement to heart and soon thousands of letters per week were being exchanged between soldiers on the front and their correspondents at home. Some soldiers wrote home themselves, some employed scribes and others still tried to teach themselves how to read and write to communicate with their friends and families.

Mail arrives at the Brigade Post Office in Linghem, France. The Indian troops' mail was censored and monitored by the British, and it is the surviving censored reports and mails that provide the most tangible sense of the Indian war-time experience.

Indian cavalry, along with two young French boys, are pictured attending to their horses in a factory that had been converted into a makeshift horse hospital.

The Indian Corps Signal Section, which was responsible for the communication requirements of the army units is pictured installing telegraph lines in Merville, France.

ON
SIGNAL
SERVICE

The personnel and baggage of a cavalry brigade are pictured on the march near Fenges, France.

The Brigade Signal Section of Dehra Dun Brigade is pictured at work in a field near St Floris, France.

STORES
SIGNALLING STORES

Facing page and above: 'L' Hindou' as the French called the Indian soldier became an integral part of life and battle on the Western Front. Indian troops were to become a common sight in the cities and towns of France for the duration of their involvement in the battlefields of France and Flanders.

Forward scouts of the 9th Hodson's Horse (Bengal Lancers), pause to consult a map.

The 20th Deccan Horse are pictured in high spirits shortly before staging an attack during the Somme offensive in July 1916. The attack was to be unsuccessful.

A regiment of Gurkhas pose in France, joined by a few French children.

A group of Sikhs pose with the children of Le Sart, a French village where they were billeted.

A group of French children watch the first line transport of a Gurkha battalion march past in Le Sart, France.

The 1/4th Gurkhas show off their kukris at a kit inspection, Le Sart, France.

A group of Gurkhas pose with their weapons near Merville, France. The men had all been wounded in the course of duty and were photographed on their return to the front.

British and Indian officers of the 18th Lancers pose for a photograph near Estrée Blanche, France.

A group of Jat soldiers engage in a wrestling match near Merville, France.

A musical party of the 6th Jats gathers for a moment of entertainment at Merville, France.

A group of Indian labourers and followers are caught on camera as they go about their normal routine at the base camp in Marseille.

Facing page and above: Indian troops decamped at Marseille on arrival in France. The pictures here give a sense of the sprawling camps, complete with horses and mules brought over for the war from India.

Indian cavalry troopers preparing a meal,
Estrée Blanche, France.

An Indian soldier carries a sheep to his camp to be killed for food.

MUSSALMANS
HINDUS
KEEP OUT

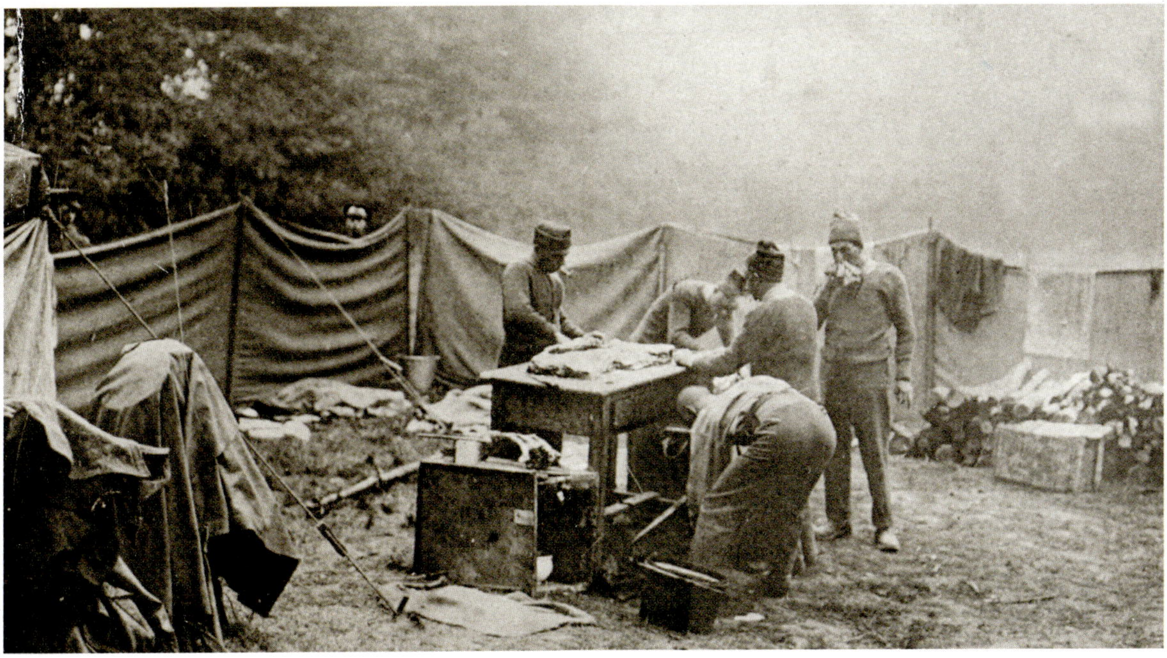

Facing page and above: Indian troops slaughter goats near Aire, France. The British paid special attention to the dietary concerns of the Indians and the picture shows two separate slaughtering pits for halal and non-halal meat. Details such as the preparation of the food and caste of the cooks were paid attention to.

Gurkhas work on a fire trench and a communication trench, near Merville, France.

A troop of Jodhpur Lancers form a firing line at Linghem, France.

9th Hodson's Horse (Bengal Lancers) lead a charge near Vraignes, France.

The 58th Rifles, Indian infantry, are pictured in the trenches at Fauquissart, France.

Indian infantry pose with early iterations of the gas mark in the trenches at Fauquissart, France.

Gurkha soldiers consolidate their capture of a trench near Merville, France.

Above and facing page: The Menin Gate, located in the Belgian town of Ypres, was unveiled as a war memorial to the Missing in 1927. It is dedicated to the British and Commonwealth soldiers who were killed in the Ypres Salient. Among some of the Indian regiments commemorated on the Gate are the 84th Punjabis, 3rd Brahmans, 4th P.A.V Rajputs, 124th Duke of Connaught's Own Baluchistan Infantry, 1st K.G.O Gurkha Rifles (The Malaun Regiment), 11th Rajputs, 127th Q.M.O Baluch Light Infantry, 14th K.G.O Ferozepore Sikhs, 15th Ludhiana Sikhs, Q.V.O Corps of Guides, 52nd Sikhs, 54th Sikhs, 129th D.C.O Baluchis, 55th Coke's Rifles (F.F.), 36th Sikhs, 47th Sikhs, Assam Military Police, 18th Infantry, 19th Punjabis, 21st Punjabis, 25th Punjabis, 31st Punjabis, 32nd Sikh Pioneers, 34th Sikh Pioneers, 35th Sikhs, 40th Pathans, 57th Wilde's Rifles (F.F.), 4th Gurkha Rifles, 17th Infantry (The Loyal Regiment) and the 9th Bhopal Infantry.

Above and facing page: The Neuve Chapelle Indian Memorial was designed by Sir Herbert Baker to commemorate the Indian soldiers who died on the Western Front in the First World War. The memorial was unveiled on 7 October 1927 by the Earl of Birkenhead, F.E. Smith, then the Secretary of State for India. The ceremony was marked by the presence of Indian troops who had been brought to France to represent the units commemorated at the memorial. The ceremonial party also included Lord Hardinge, who had ordered the Indian troops' embarkation as Viceroy of India, the Maharaja of Kapurthala, and Rudyard Kipling, who represented the Imperial War Graves Commission.

Following pages: India's contribution to the war effort in Europe was a source of endless fascination in France. The postcards on these pages show just a small range of war images featuring Indian troops and celebrating India's war contribution.

E dire che sono quelli venuti ad insegnarci la civiltà
ils sont ceux qui nous ont appris la civil
33 - GUERRE EUROPÉENNE 1914
Une petite Française souhaite la bienvenue aux soldats Hindous
Arrivée des
Boches
VIVE
FRANCE
29-1-1915
36. - GUERRE EUROPÉENNE 1914
Partie de concert par les Indiens
RÉPUBLIQUE FRANÇAISE
10
ASSOCIATION DES DAMES FRANÇAISES
" Le 14 Juillet à PARIS en 1916 " — Les Cipayes Indiens
CAPTURED AT LOOS
GERMAN TRENCH MORTAR
CAPTURED BY
39th GARHWAL RIFLES
No 4 CAPTURED GERMAN TRENCH MORTAR &

Toulouse
Troupes Hindoues — 2e Série – No 6
Le type parfait de l'Hindoue : grand, mince et muscle, remarquable par la régularité et la placidité de ses traits.
Guerre de 1914
Blessé Indien coiffant un camarade
24. GUERRE 1914 - TYPES HINDOUS
Gefangenenlager 2. Münster i. W. 1916.
Nr. 30. Groupe d'Hindous. Gurkasses.
India
Inde
GUERRE de 1914
1 - Passage des Troupes Hindoues

Some convalescent Indians sun themselves while others are chaperoned out for their march through the town and along the bracing sea front in Brighton. Brighton became the site of a number of hospitals that treated wounded Indian soldiers during the war. In this picture, the Brighton Pavilion, a 19th century orientalist kitsch palace that was used as a hospital for Indian troops from December 1914 until early 1916, can be seen in the background.

Face-to-face with Blighty

Recuperating Indian soldiers in hospitals in England

I am satisfied at being able to serve our illustrious Government body and soul and to see the countries which my ancestors never even dreamt of seeing. Now our government has issued an order that whoever will agree to serve to the end of the war will be sent over to London. This is my good fortune that I shall be able to see England and to write to my friends about it. I shall not be surprised if we have to stay there. For this we have to congratulate Government and thank them for what they have done for us. I expect to go to England within a month and I will send you a telegram whenever I arrive there. I shall learn English well there.

RAM DATT SINGH, 71ST LABOUR COMPANY, FRANCE[1]

+++

England is a fine country, but we are kept like prisoners who are in jail. All the Indians are, as it were, in jail.

LAL BADSHAH, 40TH PATHANS[2]

+++

Perhaps among the most momentous outcomes of the war for several Indian soldiers was the opportunity to see and experience England first-hand. Never before had so many Indians made a collective journey to Europe. Never again would these soldiers come so close to seeing England, the imperial ruler for whom they had risked their lives.

During the course of the war the imperial centre was to become the base where wounded Indian soldiers underwent treatment and recuperated. By early 1915 six hospitals had been established (usually by converting existing buildings) for Indian soldiers in England. Sir Walter Lawrence, who was appointed the Commissioner for Sick and Wounded Indian Soldiers in France and England in late 1914, was given the task of managing the hospital system to achieve two main aims. One was to return sepoys to the front as soon as possible. The second was to protect British 'prestige', which was usually seen to be a combination of proving to the Indian masses that British rule was just and fair and that the British ruling class' own personal behaviour was somehow beyond reproach.[3]

These aims give us a sense of the importance of the hospital sites in the Indian experience of the war. For the British authorities, they became important sites of communication and propaganda to showcase to the soldiers and a wider audience in India the care and concern that was going into the recuperation of wounded Indian soldiers. Some of the most memorable images of Indian soldiers from the war illustrate their recuperation under the ostentatious dome and chandeliers of the Brighton Pavilion, the orientalist kitsch palace built in 1823, that had become a hospital for Indian soldiers during the war. Others show Indian soldiers meeting with British dignitaries including the King himself in the vast hospital lawns. At the same time, the hospitals also became sites of contention, reinforcing the racial and sexual hierarchies of the Empire, against which Indian soldiers often chafed and even rebelled. Consequently, it was in England itself that some of the most complicated interactions between the ruler and its subjects took place during the war.

Hospitals for the wounded

The Indian Corps suffered a number of non-fatal injuries from the moment they were deployed in trenches outside Ypres in October 1914. By the beginning of December 1914, 3,915 Indian and British soldiers in the Meerut and Lahore Divisions had to be removed from the lines because of wounds. By the end of that month the number had risen to 5,860. Between October 1914, when the troops had entered battle, to December 1914, almost one in every four sepoys who had landed at Marseilles had sustained some kind of physical trauma.[4] A year later, as 1915 ended and the promise of a short war seemed a distant past, the grim reality of trench warfare had clearly set in. A soldier's letter home brings to life this destruction:

> My dear brother, great damage has [been] caused to India. Nearly two hundred thousand men have been killed. About four thousand have lost arms or legs and many have lost their sight. In India, three quarters of the population will be women and only one quarter men. Here the state of things is such that all the world over there will be two women for each man. ... All the kings have been ruined.[5]

Initially, wounded Indian soldiers were cared for in hospitals in French cities like Marseille, Boulogne or other smaller towns. However, as the war intensified and the number of wounded increased, French medical services struggled to keep up. Faced with insufficient resources and wary of the strain that transporting the soldiers would have on the railroads, the French protested that they could not accommodate the number of Indians wounded. Instead, they suggested treating the wounded men in England or Algeria. Clearly, England was a more practical option, but the possible presence of a large number of Indian troops in the country opened up a host of contradictory concerns for British authorities. On the one hand, the treatment of Indian troops in hospitals in England would allow Indian troops to be sent back to the front more quickly and bolster the British claims of being caring rulers. On the other the need to maintain prestige led to constant concerns about sexual encounters between Indian soldiers and English women as evinced by Walter Lawrence's statement, 'My one concern about these hospitals in England is the women question.'[6]

It was decided in November 1914 that all men who could not be cared for in France were to be sent to England. Still, the experience of the Indian soldiers in England continued to be shaped by the dichotomous aims of the British authorities who ensured that the Indians were provided with the best possible medical care and amenities, but also closely monitored and circumscribed the movements of the troops.

Initially, soldiers arriving in Britain were accommodated in a number of makeshift hospitals.[7] However, given the number of the wounded and the inadequate conditions of some of the hospital sites, it became increasingly clear that alternative arrangements had to be made. Unsurprisingly, when the Mayor of coastal Brighton offered the services of his city, Walter Lawrence readily accepted. Brighton was now to become one of the key sites for the medical care and recuperation of Indian soldiers during the war.

Suitable hospital locations had to be scouted in Brighton. The town's two largest hotels were identified as probable sites, but given their economic importance to the seaside town, the local authorities were reluctant to allow for their conversion. Sites like the pier and the race course were found to be unsuitable. Finally, the authorities settled on the Royal Pavilion, which had been built as a seaside pleasure retreat for the Prince of Wales (the future King George IV) in the early 1800s. The ostentatious Pavilion, which had been built in the Indo-Sarasenic style, also had the most extravagant chinoiserie interiors ever executed in the British Isles. The Pavilion's oriental domes and charming gardens enhanced its attraction as a site for recovering Indian soldiers – it was felt the Pavilion's architecture would make the soldiers feel more at ease.[8] Photographs from the time show rows upon rows of Indian soldiers recuperating in their beds under the Pavilion's great dome. The gorgeous chandeliers that hung from the ceiling probably underscored what a strange and luxurious – especially compared to any medical establishment in India – surroundings the Indian soldiers found themselves in. One Sikh soldier was so charmed that he used the famous Persian couplet inscribed on the arches of the Diwan-i-Aam in New Delhi's Red Fort to describe his surroundings, 'If there be a paradise on earth, it is this'.[9]

In addition to the Pavilion, Lawrence also procured the use of the Brighton Poor Law Institution, and a block of buildings that came to be called the 'Kitchener Hospital'. This was not only the main Indian hospital in England for the duration of the war, but also the largest military hospital in England.[10] In total six Indian Military Hospitals were established in England by early 1915. By the time these hospitals in England closed in 1916 they had treated 14,514 wounded Indians.[11]

A warm welcome

From the very beginning of the war, the British were concerned that the treatment of Indian soldiers should leave no room for complaint. Lawrence, keenly aware of the politics of treating Indian patients in England, wrote to Lord Kitchener: 'I will never lose an opportunity of impressing upon all those who are working in these hospitals that great political issues are involved in making the stay of the Indians in England as agreeable as possible.'[12] This was not just for fear of a revolt amongst the soldiers, but also to preclude the possibility of the treatment of soldiers abroad becoming rallying point for nationalists in India.

Luckily for Lawrence, the Indian soldiers were welcomed just as warmly in England as they had been in France. The first large contingent of Indian soldiers arrived at Brighton in December 1914 on a dreary, cold and rainy day. Despite the weather, crowds gathered to cheer the soldiers arriving from the front. The *Brighton Gazette* wrote:

> At last the wounded Indians are duly installed at Brighton. They arrived under rather mournful conditions. A drab day, rainstorms, and a fierce sea running in the Channel, mud-laden streets, and a vista of dripping umbrellas and mackintoshes. That was the first impression the warriors got of Brighton,

> and it was rather chilling. But crowds assembled to voice public welcome, and the reception undoubtedly cheered the brave fellows. The hundred stretcher cases in the first train that reached the terminus on Monday afternoon constituted perhaps the most distressing of the many pathetic sights seen on similar occasions during the past four months. Something akin to a feeling of awe was created by the silence with which the work of bringing them out of the train and placing them in the motor ambulances was carried on.[13]

Regardless of where they were admitted, Indian troops enjoyed good medical facilities and treatment. Lawrence noted: 'Every effort was made to keep them cheerful and provide the simple comforts, which means so much to the Indians.' It was not an effort that went in vain. One wounded Indian soldier wrote home to Peshawar simply saying, 'Do not worry about me, for I am in paradise.'[14] Another recuperating soldier, Gulab Singh, wrote to a friend: 'The arrangements for our food are excellent... The Gora Log (British) are most attentive to our wants.'[15]

The purpose of the hospitals was not just to heal, but also to make the soldiers fit for war again. The hospitals provided the patients space for exercise and drills, and amenities to make the sepoys' convalescence quick and pleasant. Soldiers were able to walk outside the hospital grounds as well (although this was usually only under supervision, reflecting the concerns the British authorities had about granting too much freedom to recuperating Indian soldiers). In the Kitchener Hospital, a large recreation room was used to project scenes of Punjab life to 'a delighted audience of soldiers from the north of India.' In Brighton, patients were allowed weekly trips to the cinema and those at the Pavilion were treated to a weekly organ recital. Gramophones regularly played the 'native airs of India' at convalescent homes and soldiers were also provided books and puzzles.[16]

Arrangements were made to ensure that the recuperating soldiers received letters sent from India and that there was distribution of vernacular papers to the patients. Patients were often taken to London on trips organized by the India Office to visit tourist attractions and famous landmarks.[17] One photograph shows a group of Indian soldiers on a tourist trip seated in a car that has a slogan 'From East to West for the Motherland' painted at the bottom. The authorities did not neglect capitalising on even a sight-seeing trip to reinforce the significance of the Indian involvement in the war effort and instill some patriotism for Britain in the Indian soldiers.

Caste and religion

This effort to keep the Indian troops happy required immense manpower and one can only wonder at the complicated bureaucracy of the hospitals. A significant number of staff were hired from India to fill service positions such as cooks, cleaners and launderers.[18] Most of the doctors chosen for the Indian hospitals had served in India previously during their careers with many drawn from the Indian Medical Service, thus ensuring that they were well aware of the cultural sensitivities involved in dealing with Indian patients. The Indian Volunteer Ambulance Corps also filled a number of positions. Mahatma Gandhi, who was in London for the latter half of 1914, helped organize the Indian Field Ambulance Training Corps and recruited almost 200 Indian students to works as dressers, orderlies, as well as intermediaries and translators between the British staff and Indian patients. As he wrote in *The Times*, 'In my humble opinion it ought to be our proud privilege to nurse the Indian soldiers back to health.'

Staffers who were Indian, or at least sensitive to the particularities of Indian customs, were essential to the smooth running of hospital operations. Particularly worried about any error made regarding caste or religious procedures, the authorities ensured that special arrangements were made for religiously segregated wards, baths, toilets, laundry services and water facilities.

The preparation of food was an especially delicate task. At the Pavilion Hospital, nine different kitchens catered to the different dietary requirements of the Indian soldiers. Not only were there different sections of the kitchen to cater to Hindus, Muslims and vegetarians, but food was also only handled, cooked and served by men of the same caste. Special arrangements were made for the killing of cattle and storing of meat, all of which was performed by butchers of the same religion or caste. The authorities also went to considerable lengths to ensure that comforting ingredients like *dal* and *ghee* were available at all hospital kitchens. This was particularly stressed after an incident in late 1914 when in the absence of *ghee*, margarine had been supplied to the wounded soldiers. The War Office promptly ordered that no margarine was to be served with the note: 'If it got about that we were using margarine, there might be an explosion similar to the old cartridge trouble of the Mutiny.'[19]

Religion was also important in day-to-day life and efforts were made to ensure that patients could worship as desired. Within the grounds of each hospital areas were allocated for different forms of religious worship. The Muslims were allowed to fast during Ramazan and appreciated the arrangements the authorities made for them.[20] The Indian Soldiers Fund provided appropriate religious texts to all the soldiers. Similar attention was placed on the funeral rites of men who had died at the hospitals in England. Hospitals provided specific storage areas and burial procedures. Despite the 1902 Cremation Act, which technically banned open-air cremation, cremation was sanctioned by the Home Office at a site near Patcham on the Downs near Brighton. Traditional funeral prayers would be conducted by the soldiers in attendance and the body cremated on one of three open-air concrete cremation slabs on this spot. After the body was burnt, the ashes would be scattered in the nearby sea with religious prayers to complete the funeral ceremonies.[21]

In total, 53 Sikh and Hindu soldiers from the Brighton hospitals were cremated at Patcham. Today the site is commemorated by a Chattri memorial with the following inscription: 'To the memory of all the Indian soldiers who gave their lives in the service of their King Emperor in the Great War this monument erected on the site of the funeral pyre where the Hindus and Sikhs who died in hospital at Brighton passed through the fire is in grateful admiration and brotherly affection dedicated.' Most of the Muslim soldiers were buried with Muslim rites and a full military firing squad at a burial site near the Shah Jahan Mosque, which had been built with the financial backing of the Begum of Bhopal and was at the time the only purpose-built mosque in England.

Honour and gratitude

These arrangements certainly went beyond what the Indian soldiers would have been accustomed to in India. There, soldiers were expected to provide their own bedding, clothing and food while in hospital. In addition, medical equipment and services were not of the same standard as in

England. Undoubtedly, the care the authorities were taking with arrangements did, to a degree, have the desired impact on inculcating the loyalty of the patients. A saddler, Ibrahim, wrote to his family in Sialkot to say:

> On the 16th December a syce belonging to our section died, and the Government made arrangements for his burial. A fine coffin was provided on which his name and age were engraved. The inside was lined with silk cloth and cushions of silk. In our country, doubtless, only the greatest in the land are furnished with coffins of this sort. He was buried in a Moslem cemetery near London with great honour and dignity. The exalted Government has showered every blessing on us here, which I shall remember all my life, and which will bind me in complete loyalty. Yesterday some royal princesses came from London to see us. They spoke to each one and treated us kindly as if we had been their children.[22]

To keep up the soldiers' spirits a number of dignitaries made visits to the hospitals, the most prominent being the King himself. During his visits the King mingled with the soldiers and also awarded bravery medals to the wounded who had received these. The Victoria Cross winner, Mir Dast, for example, received his award from the King in the hospital grounds. This direct interaction with the King acted as a great morale booster among a section of the troops. To further remind the soldiers of their devotion to the King, every Indian soldier received a picture of the King and improvements in pay and allowance in January of 1917.

Jemadar Kishan Singh's letter to his wife in Punjab, enclosing the New Year's card depicting the King, gives us a sense of the reverence many soldiers had for the monarch:

> I have sent you thrice before pictures of His Majesty. As you framed those and put them up on the wall opposite the door, so do the same with this portrait after framing it. Worship it every morning when you get up. This is an act of religious merit, and the portrait will be a memorial. Every morning, pray to the Guru that He will give victory to the King. Do not be anxious about me. I am quite happy.[23]

Another letter, from Dafadar Muhammad Husain of 36th Jacob's Horse to a friend vividly brings to life the immense gratitude many soldiers felt at the way they had been taken care of:

> I am in the English hospital. The English doctors pay great attention to the Indian sick. We get very good food, beds, etc. and I cannot sufficiently praise the building: it is a very splendid building. Old pensioned officers and their wives come to the hospital and enquire after our health, and give fruits and sweetmeats to the sick, and we also get fruit and sweetmeats from the state. May God make our King victorious; it is proper for you to pray so, too. The state of the Indian troops in the battlefield is very prosperous; they get excellent food, and you should not believe what liars say; the Germans are but 'guests of a few days', for on all four sides the English and French and Russians have enclosed them and they are very hard up for rations. How can hungry men fight? ... England is a very fine country. The King and Queen themselves came to visit the sick in hospital, and asked everyone if he had any sort of inconvenience. Every soldier blessed them and said that they were well served in every way and prayed from their Majesties' long lives.[24]

The British authorities were also keen to mould opinion amongst the soldier class at large and back in India. By 1915, every soldier who left the Brighton Pavilion Hospital was given a small booklet published in English, Gurmukhi, and Urdu, which provided a short history of the Royal Pavilion and a description of it as a hospital for Indian soldiers. Copies of the booklet were also distributed in India. The booklet acted as subtle propaganda by stressing how the soldiers were living in a Royal Palace, how the caste and religious considerations were followed and how the medical facilities available were best-in-class. Similarly, photographs of Indian soldiers convalescing under the sumptuous chandeliers and domes in the Brighton Pavilion or posing in the ample grounds of the hospital were widely circulated.[25]

Dismay and dissent

But if for some soldiers the experiences in the hospitals were enough to reaffirm their imperial loyalty this was not uniformly the case. Even by late 1914, Indian soldiers were demoralized by the prospect of returning to the trenches having recovered from their wounds.

Ragbir Singh, a Dogra with the 59th Rifles wrote to his friend in the Kangra district:

> I have been wounded twice, and now this is the third time that I am being sent to the trenches. The English say it is all right. How can it be all right! As long as one is unhurt, so long they will not let one off. If Parmeshwar allows I will escape, but the butcher does not let the goat escape.[26]

For the soldiers it was unthinkable that they were being asked to go back to the front after already suffering wounds and injury. This had never been the practice in the Indian Army. The notion that risking your life for the Emperor once was not enough and that you would have to do so again and again (until you were perhaps indeed killed) was a shocking proposition to most Indian soldiers. Mir Dast, the Victoria Cross winner, himself conveyed a request to the King that wounded soldiers be spared a return to the front. This became a talking point amongst soldiers at the hospitals. Naider Khan wrote from a hospital in England to Zaman Shah who was serving in France:

> Subedar Mir Dast sends you greetings. He has got the Victoria Cross and the King has sent for him. He wonders how he is to go to the King, because he is wounded. But he is going to make a very urgent request of the King, that a man who has once been wounded ought not to be sent back.[27]

Despite the effort taken by the authorities to mend the bodies and spirits of the soldiers, it had become clear to the soldiers that there was no respite from war, no matter how pleasant the hospital interlude. As one wounded Sikh acutely noted:

> Here I am as a King, but the war is still going on. There can be no confidence of life or of seeing again the dear children or of seeing you once more. For in a few days I shall go back to the war.[28]

Another soldier wrote home to convey the news after his examination by the medical committee that determined whether soldiers were fit to return to the front:

> Brother, I wish you all happiness. My Committee has assembled and I am to go back to the trenches. I do not at all like this, but I am helpless. The battle is very severe now but such is my fate that a bullet has not killed me. However fate is not to be relied on, and you ought to know that my family will get an allowance. I have no hope that I will come back and break bread

> with you again. I have no hope. When the regiment came here there were ten of us left. Now I am alone.[29]

In acts of defiance some sepoys tried to feign illness to avert another stint at the front and authorities noted various cases of malingering in the hospitals. Some tried putting red pigment in their urine, others simply went deaf as soon as they arrived in the hospital. Others openly complained that they were not being paid enough for the work they were being asked to do. The British dealt with these complaints through a carrot-and-stick approach. On the one hand they took strict action against malingerers, on the other they increased the soldiers' pay.[30]

Yet the general dispiritedness of the soldiers was to continue to have an impact. As the war dragged on and the body count of combatants increased there was also increasing demand on officials in India to intensify recruitment. Soldiers began writing letters to their relatives imploring them not to sign up for the war. One Pathan recuperating at Brighton wrote angrily to his brother:

> I am exceedingly displeased with you that you have left your parents and enlisted. I am very much annoyed at this.[31]

Sex and segregation

It was not just the thought of going back to the front that brewed unease amongst the soldiers. For all the efforts the British put in into making the Indians' stay in England comfortable, a clear racial segregation was always present. While acknowledging that the Indian patients would need space for fresh air, the idea of letting 'them about in the streets' on their own was an absolute anathema to the British authorities. The rules governing the passage of Indian patients from the hospital grounds to cities were strict and often inflexible. Though the rules varied in strictness by hospital, Indian soldiers were generally accompanied by white soldiers who kept an eye on them. The Kitchener Hospital, for example, was not only enclosed with barbed wire but also maintained a police guard of 45 men 'to prevent the escape of followers over the walls'.[32]

One reason for this strict policing was the fact that, perhaps even more than in France, there was fear of interracial sexual liaisons. White women were fundamental to the policing of racial borders and, consequently, the maintenance of prestige – it was not surprising that their elite status was jealously guarded.[33] The British had needed to rely on Indian soldiers for the war effort but they were acutely aware that the exercise could undermine the imperial system and were determined to prevent this. The ultimate bulwark for this was blocking Indian soldiers from forming relationships with white women. Lord Crewe, Secretary of State for India, for example, expressed his concern at the choice of Brighton as a spot for recuperating Indian patients to be based. 'Brighton seems to me a bad place, since even if 'Arry has to some extent enlisted, 'Arriet is all the more at a loose and ready to take on the Indian warrior.'

As the war progressed, sepoys also began to call the rules that circumscribed their movements into question. While very few men were punished for openly disobeying the hospital rules, some did begin to complain about the existing policies. One patient openly told Lawrence 'that the hospital resembled a prison'. In another case some men managed to make their way to a public house despite being in the charge of a trusted *havildar*.[34] Moreover, the measures taken to ensure the racial segregation soon began impacting the morale of the Indian troops. It was not a development that was lost on the British authorities. And yet, as the Indian Mail Censor noted:

> The troops in the hospital rather resent their close surveillance, but it is obviously better to keep a tight hand than allow them to conceive a wrong idea of the "*Izzat*" of the English women. A sentiment which if not properly held in check would be most detrimental to the prestige and spirit of European rule in India.[35]

Still, intimate encounters did occur. One Sikh wrote to his father to tell him how 'The English ladies ('*meman*') love me',[36] and there were instances of soldiers having illicit encounters with women. Nabi Bukhah at the Kitchener Hospital wrote:

> English girls are very free in their nature and they love Indians very much. Love making and breaking in Europe is nothing but a matter of choice, friends are plenty when purse is full.[37]

D.N. Sircar, a storekeeper at the Kitchener Hospital observed in a letter to his friend in Indore:

> The girls of this place are notorious and very fond of accosting Indians and fooling with them. They are ever ready for any purpose, and in truth they are no better than the girls of Adda Bazar of Indore.[38]

No doubt such references only added to the worry the authorities felt for the prestige of white women (and through them white men) and its being diluted by colonized men. Concern reached such a level that even the subject of white nurses in the hospitals became a loaded matter. While some hospitals did have female nurses, others did not – the commander of the Kitchener Hospital reported that 'women as nurses are unfit in an Indian unit'.[39]

It was not just the close supervision and subtly hinted sexual boundaries that the Indians occasionally chafed at and subverted, it was also the clearly racist hierarchies. All these factors – race, sex, dissent – formed a potent combination in an incident recounted in an anonymous letter by a 'Punjabi Mussalman' to Lance-Naik Aman Khan:

> One day a colonel said to a Punjabi, "You are a malingerer"... After that one or two accursed Christian ward orderlies beat the Indian soldier in such a fashion that blood ran from his fundament. After that a native officer of India brought the sepoy before the colonel commanding and pointed out that he had been thus unjustly beaten by the ward orderlies. The Colonel replied, "Subedar Saheb I cannot say anything to a white man on account of a sepoy". Now it is time to reflect. We took our oath to serve in Europe. We have crossed the seven seas and left our homes and our dear ones and our parents, and for the honour of such an unjust and false-promising King we have sacrificed our lives and now this is the honour we get in his council. No doubt before them we are regarded as inarticulate animals, but who can say that to oppress us and dishonour us is good?[40]

The letter initially created a furore and was brought to the attention of the Indian Corps Commander resulting in an enquiry. The letter was traced to Lance-Naik Abdul Hak who, it seemed, had a bullet in his brain and had undergone multiple operations. The authorities felt 'that being so, it might perhaps be best to take no notice of the indiscretion of his earlier communication but let the matter drop'. A few days following the incident,

Colonel S.H.P. Graves of the Brighton Pavilion, mentioned that the 'charges are undeserved' and offered the following explanation:

> This Abdul Hak [identified as the writer of the letter] made a great impression on the Medical Officer, latterly in charge of his ward, who took him to the Pantomime, where the Principal Boy was a very handsome young woman whose lower limbs, of which her costume allowed a complete view, were very symmetrical [. . .] I do not think I should have chosen the entertainment.[41]

If anything, the explanatory letter is even more intriguing, raising more questions about what had happened. What sort of relationship did Abdul Hak have with the medical officer? How did an evening out end up becoming a cause of such violence? Why was Abdul Hak beaten at all? None of this is clear, but it is perhaps telling that the image of a cross-dressed Principal Boy (at a pantomime a Principal Boy would be played by a woman in men's drag) hung over the whole incident pointing at both sexual and racial anxieties.

The Abdul Hak incident brings to light the many complex ways in which the colonial master and imperial subject interacted at the time of war. The war had necessitated Indian soldiers being pressed into service and fighting alongside British soldiers, but there was an underlying fear and realization on part of the British authorities that the war was challenging the rules that had helped keep the colonial system in place.

Hospitals in England became spaces for reaffirming the ideologies of imperial rule for the soldiers themselves not only for the Indian soldiers, but also audiences across the Empire. Yet, for all the effort that went into trying to make the sepoys pliant, unquestioning and grateful subjects who were at home in the imperial metropole, this very interaction with British authority also often led to soldiers contesting the policies and ideologies of imperial rule.

+++

Early post-war figures suggested that a total of **847** Indian officers, **36,310** Indian ranks, and **16,617** support staff were killed. While **1,618** officers, **62,631** Indian ranks, and **959** support staff were wounded.

The Story of Mir Dast

Most surviving images of Mir Dast are from his time recuperating at Brighton. Here, Dast is pictured posing for a portrait.

Amongst the troops sent to fight in the Second Battle of Ypres (21 April–25 May 1915) were a number of soldiers of the Indian Army. Here they joined a multiracial Allied force, comprising British, French, Canadians, Moroccans and Algerians, which was attempting to stem the onslaught of the German forces. On 26 April 1915, the Wilde's Rifles were sent as part of the Lahore Division to repair a breach in the line resulting from a German surprise gas attack on the Ypres Salient and ordered to counter-attack. The Allied artillery had failed to subdue the German forces and the troops suffered heavy losses from shells and intense rifle and machine gun fire as they advanced. Despite this, the survivors were able to reach 40 – 60 yards of the German trenches, where they were effectively stalled. As the men remained pinned down by heavy fire, nozzles resembling fire hoses appeared over the German parapets discharging green clouds of gas.

Second Ypres stands out amongst the many battles fought on the Western Front because it marked the first mass use of poison gas in battle. Warned of what to expect but without gas masks, the troops knew that they needed to dip their kerchiefs or the end of their turbans in chloride of lime or, much more distastefully, in urine and tie these over their mouths. Such measures offered minimal protection, however, and the ground was soon strewn with men writhing tortuously while the enemy increased its fire.

Among the men reeling from the effects of gas was Mir Dast, an Afridi Pathan, who attempted to rally some men and hold the line amidst the confusion and chaos of the gas attack as most of the brigade fell back. Dast and the survivors managed to hold the line till nightfall when, under the cover of darkness, they were able to withdraw. As Dast and his unit withdrew they spotted occasional abandoned survivors strewn across the battlefield. Despite suffering from the effects of gas himself, Dast helped bring eight British and Indian officers who might have otherwise died. In the process he was wounded by German gunfire. For his actions, Dast became only the fourth Indian to be awarded a Victoria Cross (VC).

Mir Dast's story is one of exemplary military service. Born into a family of Afridi Pathans on 3 December 1874 in the Maidan Valley, Tirah, in the North-West Frontier Province of British India, Dast enlisted in the army in 1894, joining the 1st Punjab Infantry (later renamed the 55th Coke's Rifles, Frontier Force). He cemented his reputation as a soldier early on, receiving the Indian General Service Medal and bar for his service during the great tribal uprising in the North-West Frontier in 1897–98. During a second stint of service on the Frontier in 1901–02, he was promoted to the rank of *naik* (corporal) and received the Waziristan bar. Another promotion to the rank of *havildar* (sergeant) followed in 1904 and Dast was awarded the Indian Order of Merit 2nd Class for gallantry in action and the Indian General Service Medal and bar when fighting in the Mohmand Campaign in 1908. As Indians were not eligible for the VC till 1911 this was the highest award for bravery attainable at the time. The next year, 1909, Dast was promoted to the commissioned rank of *jemadar*, the equivalent of lieutenant.

Following the heavy initial losses by the Indian corps in France in 1914, men were drawn from regiments in India to fill the depleted ranks on the Western Front. Dast was one of the officers cross-posted from his home unit to a regiment serving in France, serving with the 57th Wilde's Rifles, Frontier Force, in the 7th (Ferozepur) Brigade of the Lahore Division. Dast played a role in the fighting in Neuve Chapelle in March 1915 and thereafter in Second Ypres, the battle that won him his greatest renown.

Dast, along with a number of other wounded soldiers of the Lahore Division, was transferred to the Brighton Pavilion Hospital for treatment and recuperation. Writing from there to a *subedar* friend with the 57th Rifles stationed in Kohat in the North-West Frontier Province in July 1915, Dast wrote:

> I am in England. I have been twice wounded, once in the left hand, of which two fingers are powerless. The other injury is from gas – that is dhua [smoke]. I suppose you know about that. It gives me great pain and will go on doing so... The men who came from our regiment have done very well and will do so again. I want your congratulations. I have got the Victoria Cross. The Victoria Cross is a very fine thing, but this gas gives me no rest. It has done for me.

During his stay at Brighton, Dast was something of a minor celebrity being specially introduced to the Secretary of State for India, Austen Chamberlain, and Lord Kitchener during their tours of the hospital. Dast was formally presented with his VC personally by the emperor, George V, in the Pavilion grounds in August 1915, watched by a crowd of wounded Indians.

Later, Dast wrote to another friend:

> By the great, great, great kindness of God, the King with his Royal hand has given me the decoration of the Victoria Cross. God has been very gracious, very gracious, very gracious, very gracious, very, very, very, very, very [gracious] to me. Now I do not care. I want the kindness of God. If I go to Egypt, I do not regret it. The desire of my heart is accomplished. Show great zeal on your duty, and be faithful and eat the salt of the Government with loyalty.

The award of the Victoria Cross might have temporarily assuaged Dast's concerns about the issue of continued military service after injury, but it had in the past been a topic of concern for him. Having been asked by the Emperor for any specific requests, Dast's response was simple and reflected the concerns and grievances of most wounded soldiers. 'I have no son that you might give him a jemadari or havildari,' wrote Dast, 'But this is my request, that when a man has once been wounded, it is not well to take him back to the trenches. For no good work will be done by his hands, but he will spoil others' also.' The British authorities were to grant Dast's request, and in October 1915 he returned to India to re-join the 55th Coke's Rifles.

If Dast was a paragon of duty to the Crown, of some incongruity with his story is the story of his brother, Mir Mast, who also served in France as a *jemadar* with the 58th Vaughan's Rifles, Frontier Force, in the Meerut Division. On the night of 3–4 March 1915 Mir Mast, along with about twenty-four other Indian soldiers, deserted to the Germans near Neuve Chapelle. Mast had been due to receive the Indian Distinguished Medal for exemplary conduct under fire when he deserted. Rumours floated that he had been rewarded by the Kaiser with the Iron Cross for having done so. By later that year there were even reports and rumours circulating in the North-West Frontier Province that Mir Mast, along with a group of Germans and Turks, had reached Kabul and was attempting to stir up rebellion on India's borders. This was indeed true and government records tell us that while the mission to Kabul failed, Mir Mast did make it back home to Tirah where, by some accounts, he continued his involvement in anti-British activities. (For more on Mir Mast see the chapter on Indian POWs in Germany.) The story of the Mir brothers points to ways in which loyalty and dissent could often be two intertwined strains that could unravel in the political landscape of the war. If they were fighting for individual honour, glory and reward did it truly matter if these were won on the British or German side? Or perhaps in writing down his concerns about sending battle-weary soldiers back to the trenches Mir Dast had his brother on his mind. One wonders how Dast took the news of his brother's desertion, if the brothers ever met after the war and how they might have reconciled their very different approaches to imperial authority during the war.

Mir Dast is greeted by Lord Kitchener during his stay in hospital.

Mir Dast, by all accounts, continued his distinguished career in the army. In 1916 he was awarded the Order of British India, second class, which allowed him to assume the title of *bahadur* and made him one of India's most-decorated soldiers. Dast's health never fully recovered from his exposure to gas and he was transferred to pension establishment in 1917. Dast died January 1945 in Peshawar.

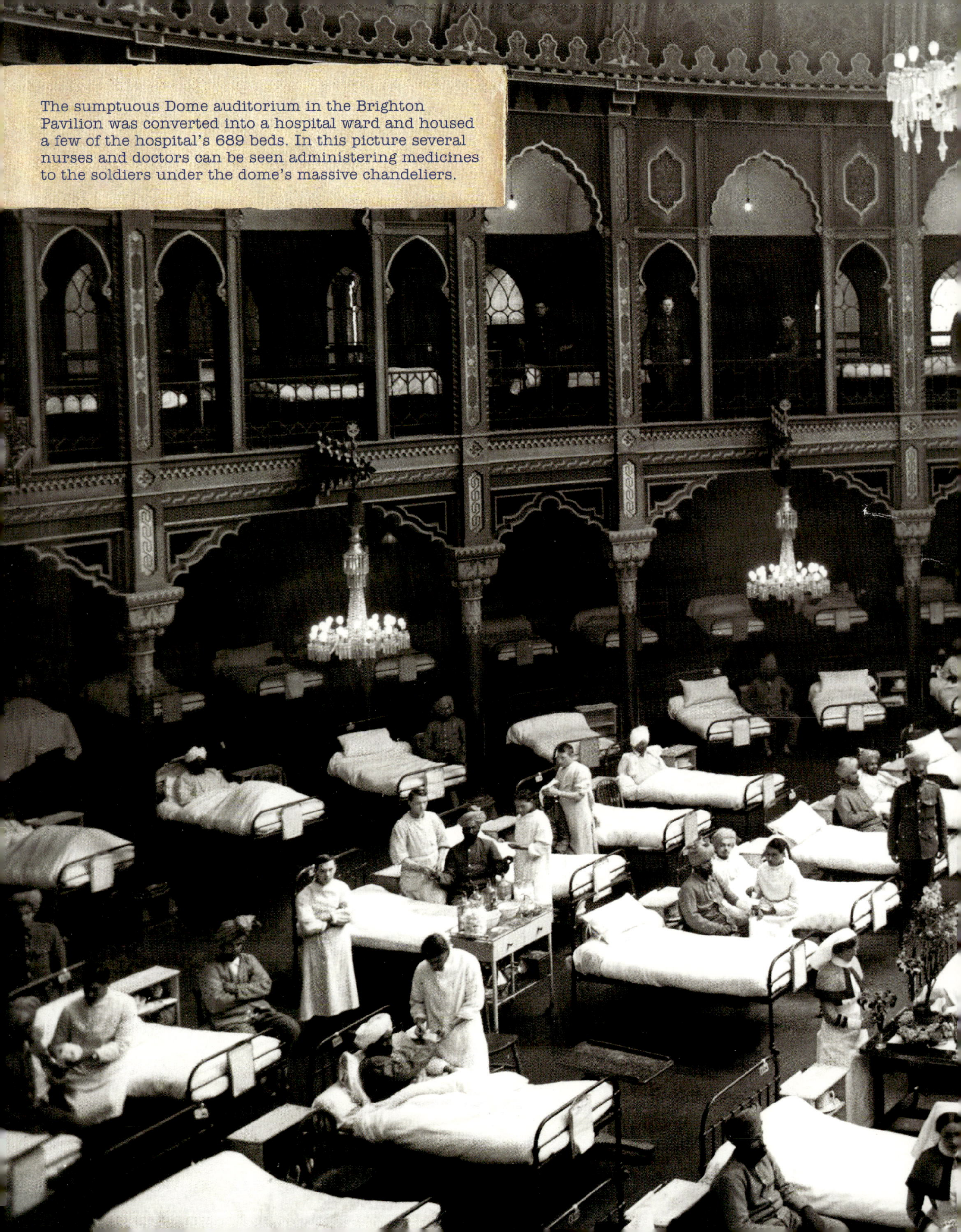

The sumptuous Dome auditorium in the Brighton Pavilion was converted into a hospital ward and housed a few of the hospital's 689 beds. In this picture several nurses and doctors can be seen administering medicines to the soldiers under the dome's massive chandeliers.

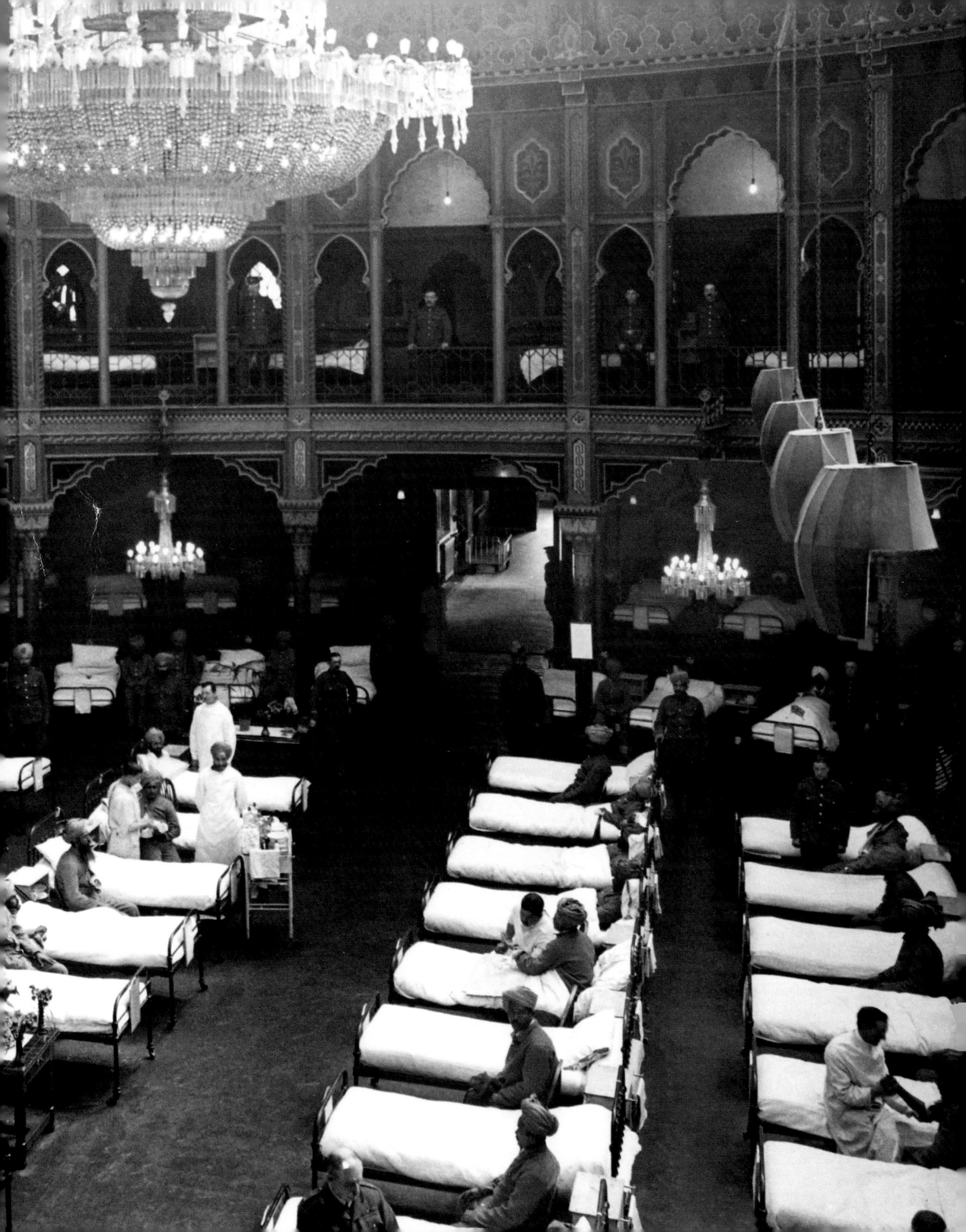

At the Pavilion Hospital, rows of tables are laid out for a tea party.

Hospital beds in the Dome ward are ready and awaiting a batch of wounded soldiers.

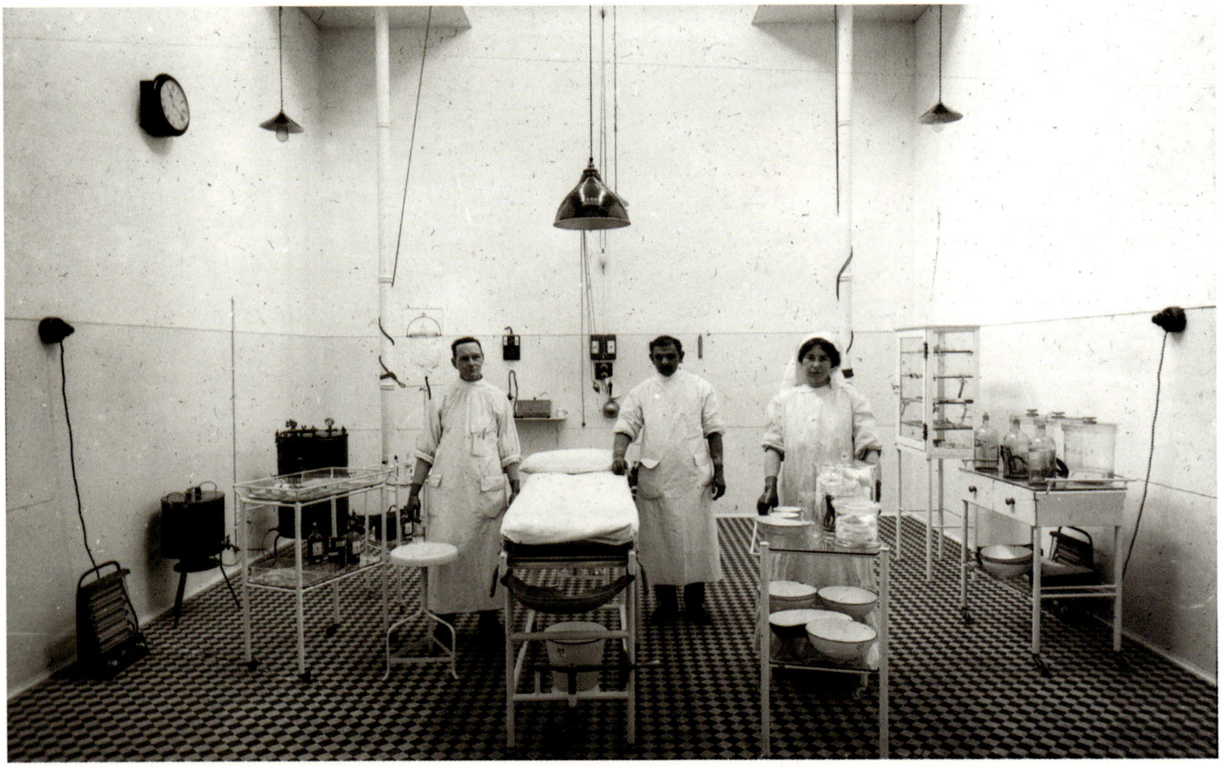

Two surgeons and a nurse are photographed in the Operating Theatre of the Pavilion Hospital.

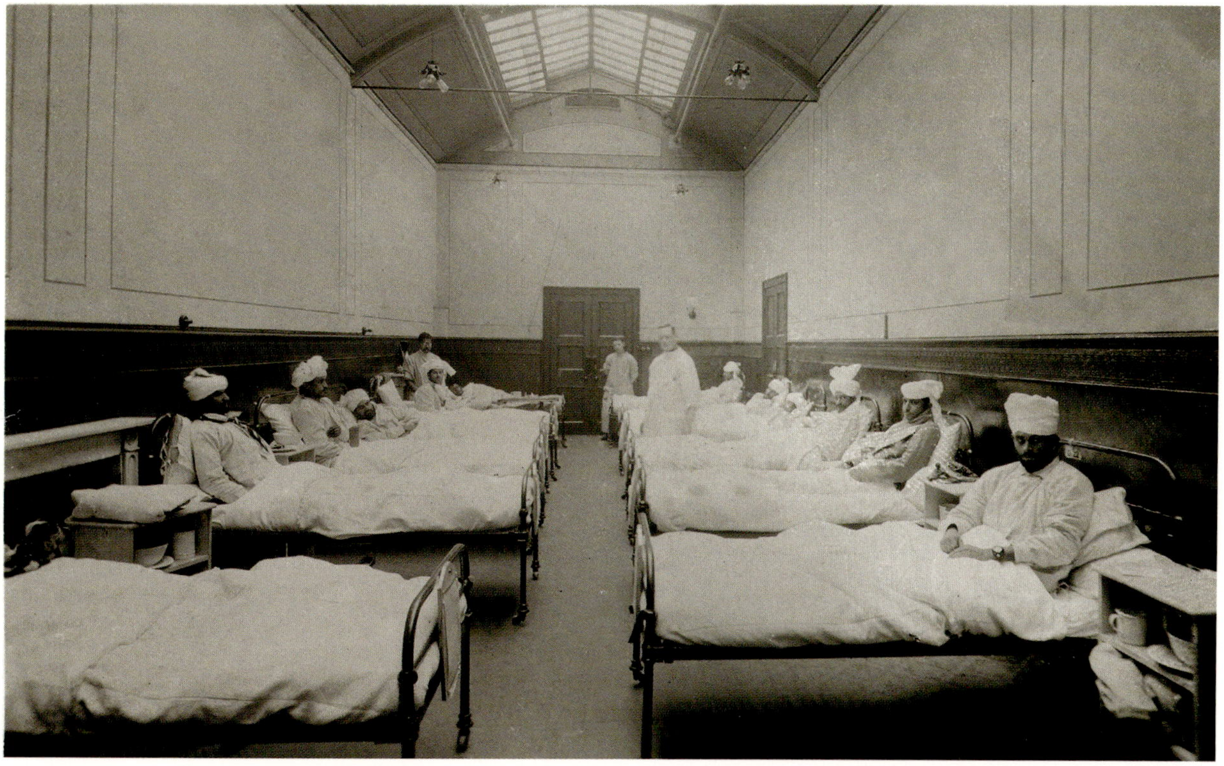

Wounded Indian soldiers recuperate in one of the several rooms of the Pavilion Hospital. This particular room was called the Masonic Room and had been given over for use by local Freemasons.

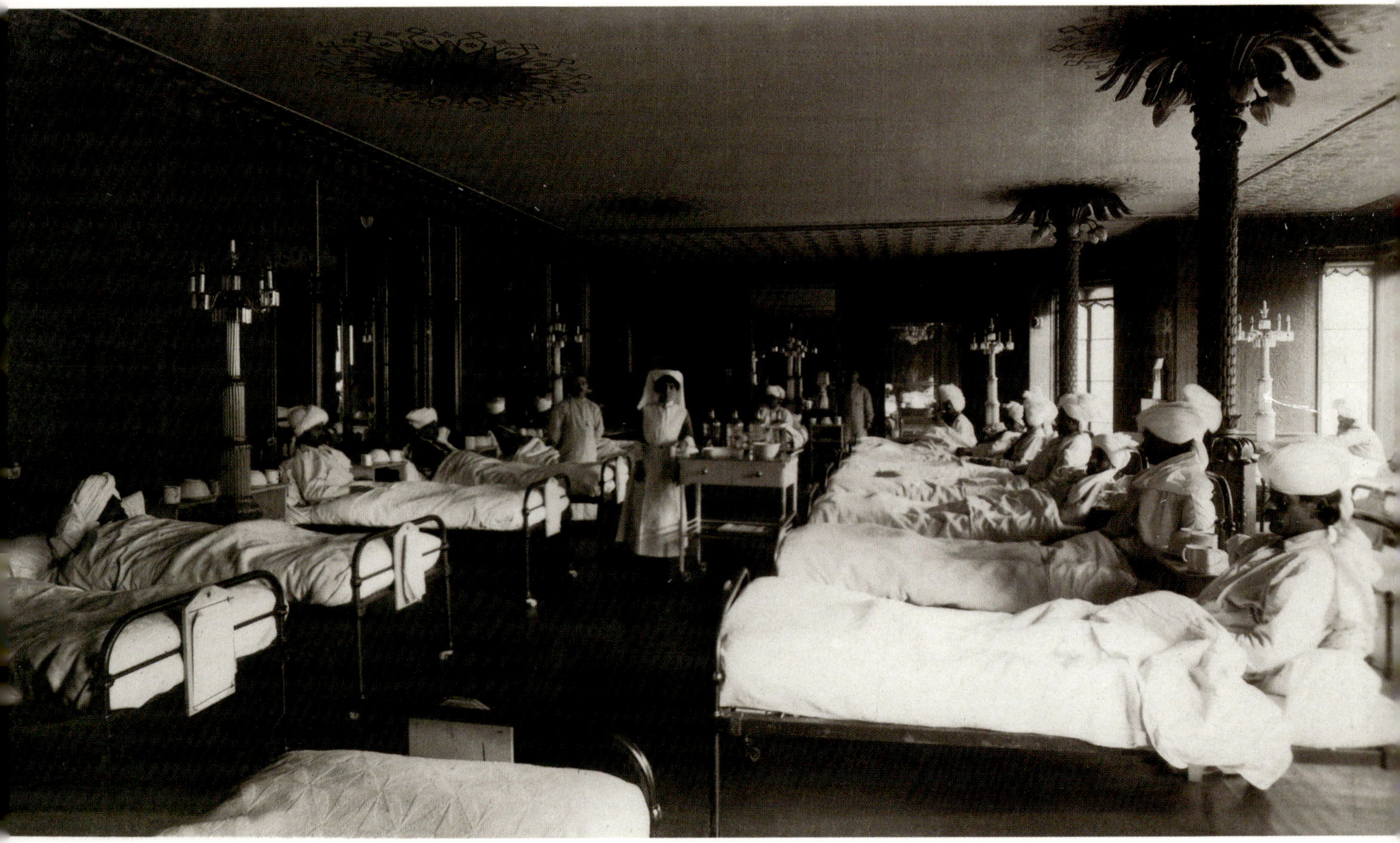

Above and facing page: Wounded Indian soldiers recuperate in one of the Pavilion's Drawing Rooms. Photographs like these were widely distributed in postcard format in a bid to showcase the excellent care the Empire was taking of its troops.

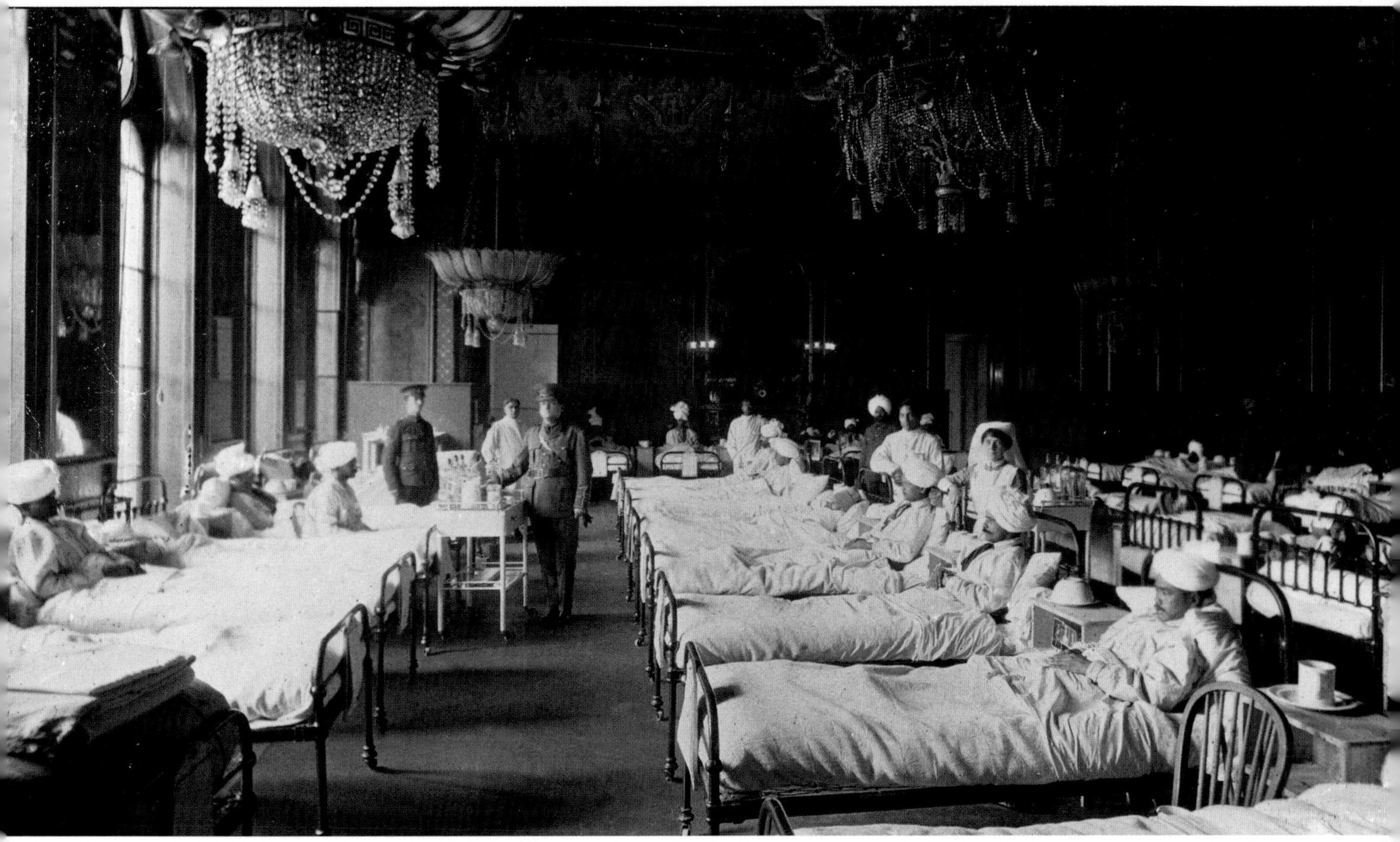

Facing page and above: Recuperating Indian soldiers lounge in the grounds of the Brighton Pavilion. The Dome can be seen in the background. Though such images create a perception of a relaxed and care-free period of reuperation, Indian soldiers were often constrained in their movements outside the hospital grounds.

The sepoys photographed here were recovering at the Brighton Hospital after having suffered extensive injuries in battle. A caption on the original photograph provides details of the pictured wounded. The sepoy seen smoking a cigarette had suffered a fractured arm and elbow caused by a German bullet. The two Gurkha soldiers, Bal Bahadur and Pim Bahadur, were cousins who were both serving with the 1/9 Gurkha Regiment. They were both wounded by the same German shell, which had killed six and wounded ten others. Pim Bahadur lost his right leg while Bal Bahadur lost his left arm and suffered a shattered thigh due to the impact of the shell. The brothers were personally visited by the Queen during their time in hospital.

A wounded Indian soldier – possibly the Victoria Cross winner, Mir Dast – is seated in a bath chair and photographed accompanied by three British troops in the grounds of the Royal Pavilion.

A group of wounded Indian soldiers enjoy a concert in the Pavilion grounds at Brighton. A Scotch piper playing the bagpipes can be seen in the foreground. At the back, a British officer has his hands on a barely visible gramophone that was also often used to keep the troops entertained.

Indian soldiers engage in a game of cards in the hospital grounds in Brighton. They are observed by a group of white medical orderlies. Contemporary accounts of the Pavilion Hospital often emphasized the Indians' fondness for games and such images showing the Indians at ease became popular postcards at the time.

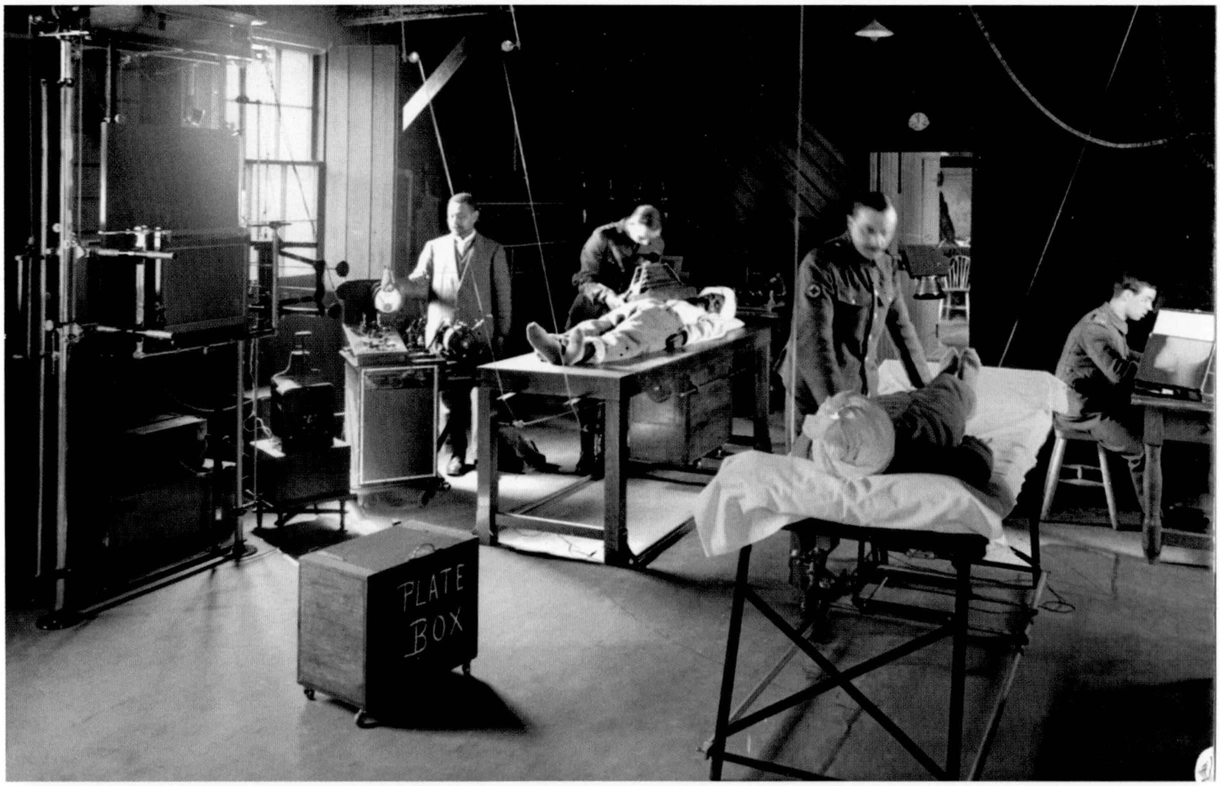
PLATE
BOX

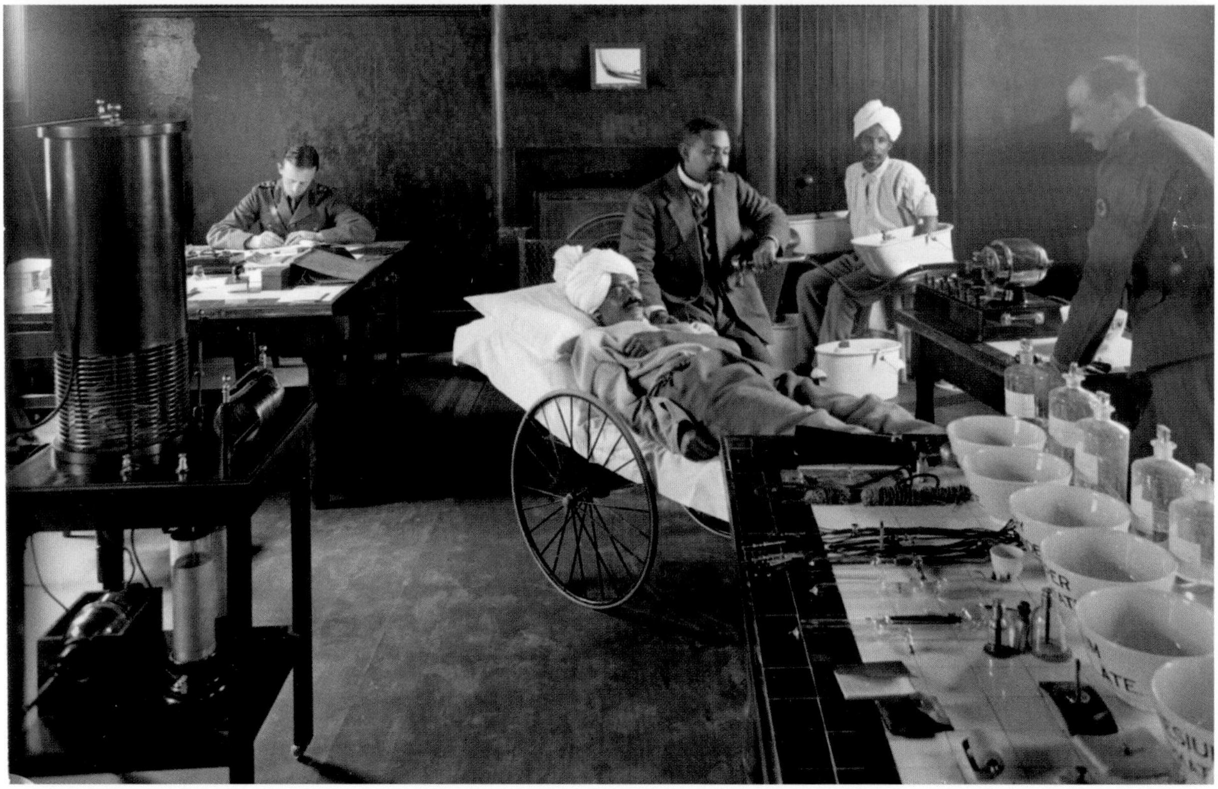

Facing page: The hospitals in England exposed Indian soldiers to advanced medical care of a kind they had probably not seen before. The image on top shows soldiers being examined in the X-ray room of the Kitchener Hospital. The image below shows sepoys receiving electric and galvanic treatment. These treatments were used for conditions such as rheumatism and sciatica which a number of Indian troops suffered from in the cold winter.

Above: A group of civilians and wounded soldiers at the entrance of the Kitchener Hospital in 1916. It was the largest of the three Indian hospitals set up in Brighton. When it opened in January 1915, it had over 1,700 beds and if necessary 1,000 more patients could be accommodated in tents or huts on the adjacent ground of the racecourse.

Indian soldiers meeting officers and dignitaries in the Royal Pavilion Gardens. The Brighton hospitals and their Indian wounded received a steady stream of visitors throughout their existence. These visits satisfied the curious public, but were even more important as propaganda vehicles in the fight to counter anti-British sentiment both in India and being promoted by the Germans and their allies and directed towards the fighting Indian soldiers in France. The most prominent visitor to the Brighton hospitals were King George V and Queen Mary who visited the Pavilion a few times. Others like Lord Kitchener, the Secretary of State for War, and the Secretary of State for India, Austen Chamberlain, also visited.

A British officer in the grounds of the Kitchener Hospital offers Indian soldiers cigarettes. Images like this were employed by the British authorities to showcase the generosity and equality with which they were looking after the Indian troops in Britain.

Convalescent sepoys at Brighton enjoying the sunny hours in the spacious grounds of the Pavilion. It is likely that they had gathered for one of the musical performances that became a feature of life in the Pavilion Hospital.

HINDOO
MEAT HOUSE

Facing page and above: Separate butchers and places for killing and storing meat were provided at the hospitals as Muslims ate Halal meat, while meat-eating Sikhs were prohibited by their religion from eating Halal, and the Hindus required their own facilities to avoid 'contamination' of the meat. Each hospital also had separate kitchens (and kitchen staff) to cater to the specific religious demands of the soldiers. The images here show the separate 'Hindoo' and 'Mohammedan' meat houses.

Indian soldiers seated in an open top bus head for a tour of Brighton. The text painted on the side of the bus reads; 'From East to West for the Motherland'. The image was taken in front of the Queen Victoria statue on Grand Avenue, Hove in Brighton.

EAST TO WEST FOR
E MOTHERLAND.

SPEED. 12 M.P.H

A group of Indian wounded at the Mount Dore Hospital in Bournemouth head out for a motor ride.

An 'Indian Gate' was added to the Pavilion structure in 1921 as a gift from India to the people of Brighton, as thanks for the care offered to the wounded Indian soldiers of the First World War. The gate was unveiled by Maharaja Bhupinder Singh of Patiala (seen in picture below) in 1921.

Slightly outside of the Brighton city centre was a site where a number of Hindu and Sikh war dead were cremated. The site was chosen to be home to a permanent memorial, which was built in the style of the traditional Indian *chattri*. The *chattri* memorial was unveiled in 1921 by the Prince of Wales to honour the contribution made by the Indian Army during the First World War.

The experience of Indian prisoners in Germany is one of the more strange episodes of the war. The Germans, with the help of Indian revolutionaries in Berlin, employed many forms of propaganda to turn the loyalties of the Indian troops. The POW camps in Germany also became rich sites for German ethnographers and linguists to conduct their research, as a consequence of which, some of the most haunting voices of Indian soldiers still survive.

In the Land of Hajji Wilhelm
Indian Prisoners of War in Germany

I see in the local press of the 5th instant a telegram from Berlin stating that the German Government intends to concentrate all Mussulman (Mohamedan) prisoners at Zossen near Berlin, where a special mosque is to be built. In view of the harsh (to use no stronger term) treatment meted out to prisoners of war in Germany, and especially to Britishers, the above information is rather symptomatic and in my opinion means that the German Authorities are trying to start an anti-British crusade amongst native officers and men of the Indian Army now in captivity.

British Consul General in Rotterdam, 15 January 1915[1]

+++

The attack in the war of the 14th year,
The world is shocked at the event.
It was summer then
And the atmosphere made it hot too.
At least provide me with a fan for some air.
I do not wish to live in Europe,
Please reach me to India.

Jasbahadur Rai, recorded at the Prisoner of War camp in Wünsdorf[2]

+++

Housed in Berlin's prestigious Humboldt University is the *Lautarchiv*, a unique sound archive comprised of more than 2,000 sound recordings made in German POW camps during the First World War. One of the recordings in the collection is that of an Indian soldier who was a POW in Germany. At 12.10 pm on 3 January 1917 the prisoner Chotte Singh spoke into a phonogram to recite a snatch of a *bhajan* about the god Ram, *'Raghubar Kausalya ke laal'.* To a listener today there is an immediacy to his voice that belies the hundred years that have passed since he spoke these words. Having recited the verse, Chotte Singh adds this:

> Soldier Chotte Singh.
> District Fatehpur.
> Village Kaumdar.
> I am imprisoned in Germany in the war of 1914.
> The German Badshah is looking after me very well; I live in great comfort.
> Jai ho! Jai ho! Jai ho!
> He then lets out a hearty laugh.[3]

Chotte Singh is only one of the thousands of human voices that populate the *Lautarchiv*.

The recordings represent the work of the Royal Prussian Phonographic Commission, which was active between 1915 and 1918 and was envisioned by its founder the philologist Wilhelm Doegen as a museum of voices from around the world. The project was made possible by the fact that Germany during the war became home to a number of POWs from a variety of continents and of different ethnicities and races. It was a ripe sample set for linguistic study.[4] While there was no official agreement on the number of Indian POWs in Germany, the number was believed to be between 1,500 to 2,000.[5] These Indian POWs lent their voices to some of the recordings that can still be found in the archive today.

For the German philologists the personal stories of their objects of study held little interest. The prisoners usually had to read out aloud from an agreed-upon text. This could be a recitation of standardized list of words, alphabets, numbers, fairy tales or religious texts. As linguistic specimens these recording were to have no unaccounted for deviations. And yet, occasionally the recordings hint at the lived experiences of these soldiers who found themselves prisoners of the Kaiser.[6]

Chotte Singh's is just one of the many voices that populate the *Lautarchiv* – voices that tell snatches of stories which sadly have no neat conclusion. Did Chotte Singh make it back to India? What happened to him? Was he truly happy in Germany or are his words just posture and propaganda? What were the politics of Germany's interaction with these prisoners? These are questions that his brief words from a hundred years ago provoke, but unfortunately do not answer.

The racialization of the battlefield

The novelty of fighting in the battlefields of Europe gripped not just the colonial troops, but also greatly impacted European imaginations, not just British and French, but German as well. For the German and Indian troops both fear and fetishisation impacted conceptions of the other.

The Germans vigorously protested against the use of African and Asian soldiers (and it should be stressed here that the racial biases against Africans were much more pronounced) in Europe for the very same reason that the British had once invoked in the past, before military necessity led to the muting of such fears – it was seen as a breach of 'racial etiquette'.[7] This objection to colonial troops fighting Europeans became a central plan in Germany's propagandist attempts to generate outrage, at least amongst neutral countries such as Italy, Romania and even the USA, against the violation of the racial order and to make Germany a sympathetic party. It was alleged that the use of colonial troops would impact on the future of the colonial system and the supremacy of the 'white race'. If colonial troops were trained in the handling of modern arms, if they were brought to Europe and saw the white nations fighting against each other, and if they were even allowed to participate in these battles and experience the vulnerability of the white man, they would lose their respect once and forever. After the war, they would turn their weapons against their own masters and revolt against colonial rule. German propaganda argued that this flagrant breach of white solidarity should be condemned by every civilized nation.[8]

In Germany, colonial troops were represented as nothing short of beasts. In the summer of 1915, the German Foreign Office put into circulation a pamphlet with the title 'Employment, Contrary to International Law, of Coloured Troops upon the European Theatre of War by England and France', in which many atrocities were attributed to colonial soldiers, such as the poking out of eyes and the cutting off of the ears, noses and heads of wounded and captured German soldiers.[9] The writer Hans Friedrich Blunck, who had volunteered for the war and was to later become a leading cultural figure in the Nazi regime, wrote:

> The enemy deployed Senegalese negroes and Indian auxiliaries against our glorious volunteers, and it was as if this trembling, beastly smell of dark-coloured peoples emerged from the steam of blood that covered the battlefield. As if, with the inferior blood of these strangers, something poured into the soil to plague the country, as if the earth knew it would never be green again...[10]

If on the one hand colonial troops became a topic of racial propaganda that aimed to provoke German and non-aligned European sensibilities, on the other they were also pictured as victims of their colonial rulers. The *Continental Times* featured an editorial in February 1915 reminding readers that the English, who refused to travel in the same railway car with a coloured person had already pressed some 200,000 'heathen mercenaries' into service to fight against Germany. The paper also argued that the appalling losses of Indian and African troops in northern France and Flanders, as compared to those of the English, 'gives substantial evidence that John Bull is true to his old traditions in utilizing other races to do his hard fighting.' A columnist of the paper asked rhetorically, 'Is it a sign of progress in culture and civilization worthy of the 20th century, to drag these guileless Hindoos thousands of miles across sea and land, to drive them into the firing lines on the battlefields of Europe against the first soldiers of the world [?] Such action is the acme of cruelty. Cruelty, not against the German soldiers, for I knew their sentiments towards their Indian adversaries: Contempt and Pity!'[11] This dichotomy of opinion helps us better understand how the Germans appealed different sentiments where relevant. Once Indian POWs were captured, concerns about racial purity took a backseat and anti-British rhetoric like this was heavily employed to turn the Indian soldiers against their colonial masters.

If simplistic notions informed German opinions of Indians, Indian soldiers, who were heading off to Europe, too did not feel any great sense of solidarity with the Germans. If anything, the primary emotions the Germans stirred up in Indian soldiers fresh in the battlefields of Europe were fear and concern. Even before Indian troops had reached the battlefields of Flanders, the Punjabi newspaper *Paisa Akhbar* reported a 'rumour that the Germans have cut off the heads of some Gurkha and Sikh soldiers and have sent them to the Powers with the complaint that the English are sending Indian soldiers to the front.'[12] The *Dipak* proclaimed 'Indians, tender-hearted as they are, have been greatly moved by German atrocities in Belgium and shrink from setting eyes on the German demons.'[13]A war song ascribed to Subedar Ajit Singh Rawatt conveys the standing the Germans had assumed in the Indian imagination:

> Everyone says German, German. The name of God has thus been forgotten. People only talk of the German. The German, he is the meanest of all

> belligerents. Extirpate his brood altogether. The German. He is an infidel, he is absolutely without sense of shame. He has no "Dion" and no "Dharam". The German is the vilest creature in the universe; no one is pleased with him. He whom people designate German is a great scoundrel, a veritable pest. The German, we call him the "Hun". Oh Lord, grant this race be extinct. Come what may finish with him here and now. Come, muster together ye heroes; let us all go to the field of battle. The limit which fate set to his life has arrived. He has done a deed the effect of which will be the effacement of his name and of his existence in history. He will be reduced to the plight of a half-naked helot. Sing, Jemadar Gulah sing, "May our King be ever victorious".[14]

For the nationalist press in India, the fact that Indian soldiers were taking on such a brutal enemy only pointed out the hollowness of these racial hierarchies that placed the white man above all other people. As early as November 1914, the *Paisa Akhbar* argued that the bravery shown by Indian troops would 'win for India the honour she deserves among the nations of the world'. For the newspaper the heavy casualty rate of Indian troops in the war would be made up by this 'rich reward'.[15]

The *Tribune* went a step further writing in early 1915:

> If there is one fact more than another which emerges from the war it is that a large portion of the German nation – white people, par excellence – live on an ethical level with the Huns and possess the moral evils of the Zulus and the Mami. That is the plain English of the doctrine of "frightfulness". The inhuman atrocities in Belgium and France proclaim to all the world the downfall of all theories of inherent moral pre-eminence of the white race.[16]

This was exactly the sort of subversive disregard for racial hierarchies that the Germans argued the use of colonial troops would generate (and indeed, this was the sort of rhetoric that still bothered at least some Britons, despite the use of colonial troops in Europe).

Yet, despite these highly charged, race-tinged perceptions, the realpolitik of the war also meant that inter-imperial rivalry was a bigger driver of propaganda and policy. No doubt, the Germans were genuinely distraught at the use of colonial soldiers in Europe. But they were also keen to make propagandist use of captured sepoys and realized that these very soldiers could be useful if the Germans treated them obligingly when they were captured.[17] The possibility of turning Indian soldiers and employing them against the British was a prospect so tantalising that even racial concerns were kept aside in pursuit of this aim. For Indian soldiers too this imperial rivalry also opened up spaces for them to dissent and show surprising instances of agency against their colonial rulers.

Revolutionizing India

For Germany, India was not just Britain's most valuable colony but also its most vulnerable asset. This belief was articulated in the strongest terms by Kaiser Wilhelm at the end of July 1914 when British neutrality in an impending war became a dead letter:

> Now this entire structure must be ruthlessly exposed and the mask of Christian peacefulness be publicly torn away... Our consuls in Turkey and India, our agents, etc., must rouse the whole Muslim world into wild rebellion against this hateful, mendacious, unprincipled nation of shopkeepers; if we are going to shed our blood, England must at least lose India.[18]

The Kaiser's chief of general staff, Helmuth von Moltke, agreed with the assessment, writing on 2 August 1914, before a full-fledged breakout of war, to the German Foreign Office calling for revolution in India, the heart of the Empire, and Egypt, which connected large chunks of the Empire to London via the Suez Canal.[19] The German trump card for setting off this series of revolutions was Islam. Germany had just concluded a secret treaty with the Ottoman Empire and Moltke believed that 'the treaty with Turkey will make it possible for the Foreign Office to realize the idea and to awaken the fanaticism of Islam.'[20]

This was not as far fetched an idea as it might seem today. Even before France, Britain and Russia had joined together in the Triple Entente of 1907, Germany had begun sizing up the potential coalition of enemies that was slowly encircling it. They each had a massive Achilles Heel – millions of unruly Muslim subjects whose resentment at being dictated to by infidels could potentially be inflamed.[21] It is worth highlighting that in 1914 out of 270 million Muslims in the world, 100 million were British subjects (making Britain the largest Muslim Empire in the world); 20 million each were under French and Russian rule.[22]

The cultivation of the Ottoman Empire (and through it the Muslim populations across the world) was a policy that had been pursued by Germany since the turn of the century and the war only marked a moment when German efforts could come into fruition.[23] The Ottoman Sultan still held the title of Caliph and the Germans hoped that his call for jihad would rally Muslims across the world, especially those who were subjects of the enemy country. In British India, the Sultan-Caliph had already proved to be a rallying point and focus of anxiety for Indian Muslims during the Balkan wars (1912–1913) and German diplomats were eagerly reporting on the Muslim rage surging through India.[24] In time the Germans were to discover that these reports were exaggerated and that Islam was not the rallying cry they had assumed it to be, but for now the vision of rebellion in India was tempting enough to demand serious pursuit.

Germany's India policy during the war was largely the brainchild of the orientalist scholar Max Frieherr von Oppenheim.[25] Oppenheim, a son of the Oppenheim banking dynasty, combined a career in diplomacy and Orientalist scholarship and became responsible for issues regarding the Orient and India in the German Foreign Office. In his 1914 'Memorandum on revolutionising the Islamic territories of our enemies', Oppenheim argued that Indian prisoners, Hindus, Sikhs, and Muslims, must be indoctrinated without delay against their English colonial masters, because 'of the countries to be revolutionized', India was 'by far the most important in terms of the ultimate success of the war'.[26] These efforts were organized mainly by the German Foreign Office's Information Centre for the Orient (Nachrichtenstelle für den Orient, NfO) whose operations were meant to impact public opinion in the colonies and spread propaganda among colonial troops and POWs. Oppenheim, who had proposed the NfO as a special bureau to deal with propaganda efforts aimed at the Orient, was its first chairman.

The German alliance with the Ottoman Empire and Germany's willingness to support movements opposing its enemy's colonial presence made Berlin not just a gathering place for all kinds of pan-Islamists but also a number of anti-British revolutionaries. Particularly keen to help Germany in its efforts to spread revolution in India was the Indian Independence Committee (IIC). The Committee, formed in 1914, comprised Indian students and émigrés residing in Germany and famously included important Indian revolutionaries and Gadharites such as Har Dayal, Maulavi Barakatullah, Virendranath Chattopadhyay (brother of the Indian nationalist, Sarojini Naidu), and Raja Mahendra Pratap amongst others who championed the cause of Indian independence.[27]

The IIC propagated the view that revolt was imminent in India, especially since the British would be forced to commit most of their military manpower in the country to the war effort thus leaving their position in India itself weak. They also tried to convince the Kaiser that it would be possible to enter India with an Indian battalion through Afghanistan. By the end of 1914, the NfO and the IIC had decided on various actionable initiatives. Some Indians would go to the Persian Gulf to convince Indian troops there not to fight the Turks. Another group would head to Afghanistan and, with the help of Indians living there, conduct propaganda within India itself. A third group of emigrants would remain in Berlin and carry out propaganda activities targeting soldiers fighting on the Western Front and among the captured POWs.[28]

Breeding dissent

As early as November of 1914, German airplanes began dropping propaganda leaflets over British trenches on the Western Front in a bid to get Indian soldiers and in particular Indian Muslim soldiers, who made up roughly 30 per cent of the Indian Army, to defect. One read, 'The Sheikh ul-Islam had proclaimed a Jehad (holy war) on the Id day at Mecca against the British, the Russians and the French. The Sultan has commenced the war against the oppressive British, Russians and French and he has been joined by the Afghans.'[29] The German authorities also tried hard to inculcate the belief that Indian soldiers had a better chance of survival under the Germans than the British. One North African Muslim deserter stressed in one of these leaflets how 'We have a duty to mention with gratitude the care that has been shown towards Muslim prisoners by the Germans – the true friends and protectors of Islam.'

The Kaiser had already acquired the moniker *Hajji* Wilhelm after his tour of the Middle East in 1898 and the rumours spread not just about the Kaiser being a friend of Muslims but also having perhaps converted to Islam himself. In February 1915, a Pathan in the 55th Rifles at Kohat wrote to a friend serving in France with the 58th Rifles:

> Remember this one thing, that the Sultan Badshah is one of us. We hear that the German Badshah has become a Mussulman. You are a wise man, understand and think over this. Then draw your own conclusion. Islam is a good thing. You are out of reach nor can we help you. But we pray much.[30]

If appealing to their religious sentiments was one way to strike a nerve with Muslim soldiers, it was not the only appeal the Germans tried to make. Some propaganda appealed more to the nationalist sentiments of the Indian soldiers. The IIC activists helped the German Army Command in France with revolutionary leaflets that called on soldiers to fight against English rule of India. In late February 1915, the Germans planted literature to incite disloyalty written in Urdu and Gurmukhi in glass bottles in front of the Indian lines.[31] An appeal written by Har Dayal in the early months of the war addressed to 'Ye brave warriors of India!' argued:

> You have been deceived. You are meant to fight here, on foreign soil for the British who keep your home country in subjugation. But you do not know that at this moment your people themselves have risen against the English and want to win their freedom ... The English hide this information from you. ... But ... The Germans do not want to kill you with their terrible weapons. They love your country and are well disposed towards you ... Although you cannot participate in the freedom fight of your brothers as you are here in a foreign country, you can help them by not fighting for their enemies here. In the battle, throw down your weapons and give yourselves up to the Germans![32]

Worried about the impact no news at all would have on the morale of the Indian troops the British authorities did occasionally allow some letters from Germany to reach their intended recipients. Many of them conveyed a sense of well being that would no doubt have pleased the German authorities. Makhan Singh, a clerk in the 47th Sikhs serving in France wrote to his sister in India to say:

> My sister, I write with sorrow that Harnam Singh is a prisoner in the enemy's country. News of this will have reached you beforehand. We have heard that six men of our regiment are prisoners in Germany. They are quite well and happy, because the Germans deal very lovingly with the men of India & treat them very well. Now he is in no danger of his life.[33]

There is no doubt that this propaganda coupled with news from POWs in Germany played on the minds of the sepoys, especially as the war stretched out and they wondered if the Germans did offer them the best way out of the bad situation they had found themselves in.

Cases of desertion occurred periodically throughout the war, particularly amongst the infantry, despite it being a risky course of action and some soldiers did succeed in reaching enemy lines safely.[34] The most famous case took place on 2-3 March 1915 when 23 Afridi sepoys belonging to the 58th Rifles abandoned their posts to desert to the Germans. The 58th had been involved in some of the worst fighting on the Western Front. From end October through November and December 1914, the men had fought without a break for large periods of time and with high casualty rates. The regiment spent most of January 1915 recuperating but returned to the front in February with likely involvement in forthcoming offensives.[35] One can only imagine the toll the war had taken on these men who had so far not shied from battle – Jemadar Mir Mast (brother of the Victoria Cross winner Mir Dast) and Sepoy Azam Khan were due to receive the Indian Distinguished Medal for exemplary conduct under fire when they deserted. At this point desertion probably offered a better chance of survival than a forthcoming battle. The propaganda the Germans had been sowing had clearly played a part in the desertion. The men had heard of the Ottoman alliance and that the Germans treated Indian prisoners well. Such news motivated them to send one of their party across no-man's-land with a German propaganda leaflet to verify their claims. Once satisfied, the man signalled – by whistling three times – for the others to desert.[36]

In Germany, these men articulated their grievances. Not only were they upset about the casualties and injuries suffered in battle, they also resented the meagre Rs.11 a month they were paid, noting that the sum was not enough for them to betray their religion. The men said that they wanted their rifles back so that they could go to Afghanistan to fight alongside the Turks against the English.[37] It is not unlikely that a number of these grievances were indeed genuine (even Mir Dast articulated concerns about returning to the front after injury to the King himself upon being awarded the Victoria Cross) and provided the foundations for disenchantment that German propaganda could exploit. It is also just as possible that the soldiers were telling the German authorities what they wanted to hear. After all, cooperating enthusiastically with the Germans would only ensure good treatment for the deserters and offer a decent chance of returning home. It is telling that actual attempts at a proper mission to India and plans to ferment rebellion did not amount to much, either in Germany or in the Ottoman Empire. Mir Mast joined an ambitious German mission to Kabul that aimed to convince the Emir to abandon neutrality, side with the Central Powers and invade India. The Emir stalled once the mission reached Kabul.[38] Unsurprisingly, the British had increased the Emir's annual stipend giving him little reason to rebel for the time being. Mir Mast, having negotiated with considerable success the wartime political landscape, returned home to Tirah.[39]

POW camps

German propaganda was not only aimed at provoking desertions amongst Indian soldiers, it also aimed to turn the loyalties of captured Indian soldiers. Indian soldiers who were taken prisoner on the Western Front were first brought to the French town of Lille and from there sent to German POW camps. From their arrival in Lille itself the propaganda efforts were made by the NfO and IIC. Soldiers were asked about the deployment of troops and efforts were made to convince the soldiers to return to the British lines to convince other sepoys to desert.[40]

Most Indian POWs were interned in the so-called Halfmoon Camp at Wünsdorf, which had been erected in January 1915 expressly for colonial Muslim POWs. The Indian soldiers were confined to a section of the camp that came to be called *Inderlager* – the Indian camp. The NfO was keenly aware that the POWs would have to be treated carefully if Germany wanted to gain any traction with them. It noted that Indian troops came from many races or 'nationalities'. Each had specific dietary and cultural concerns about which they were 'extremely sensitive' and, therefore, care had to be taken to avoid 'anything that might offend their sense of honour.'[41]

The most visible symbol of catering to the prisoners' cultural needs was a wooden mosque built on the premises of the Halfmoon Camp. The mosque had the distinction of being the first built for solely religious purposes in Germany. The British authorities noticed that Indian POWs at the camp often sent picture postcards of the mosque to their relatives and friends and drily observed, 'Carefully read and scrutinized, all this correspondence appears harmless, and in this connection it would be interesting to learn whether the pious Germans are in the habit of building churches for all their prisoners... It is evident Germany is making every effort to win the sympathy of the Indian prisoner for propaganda purposes... it appears the most attention is paid to Mahomedens and Sikhs who are most frequently photographed.'[42]

Further efforts in this propaganda included allowing prisoners to celebrate religious festivals (Bayram for Muslims and Holi and Fagu Purnima for Hindus were particularly big events) and to slaughter and prepare their own meat.[43] Proper arrangements had to be made for prisoners who had died in captivity – Muslims were to be given their own burial place; Hindus would have their remains burned. The prisoners were entertained with slide shows, films, and even taken on tours of Berlin and musical instruments were procured for them to perform. There is striking similarity in the efforts of the Germans to win over Indian POWs to the methods used by the British who were at pains to ensure that there was little room for complaint on religious or other grounds for recuperating Indian soldiers in England. In a bid to ensure German propaganda did not win out British agencies like the Indian Soldiers Fund ensured that Indian POWs were in no way ignored, sending them gifts and care parcels aplenty.[44] Both powers understood the importance the effect such measures had on the mood of the Indian soldiers and their receptiveness to propaganda. This awareness was displayed by no less that the Kaiser himself. Ram Nath Singh, a sepoy of the 9th Bhopal Infantry was captured by the Germans in December 1914 and had an encounter with the Kaiser while recuperating in a German hospital:

> The Kaiser... enquired through the vazier whether in my judgement his hospital and the arrangements thereof were not superior to an English hospital. Being a prisoner in his hands and therefore completely under his thumbs I was obliged to give a reply that would tickle his vanity and please him.[45]

To further its propaganda efforts amongst POWs the NfO put forward the idea of publishing a camp newspaper called *El Dschihad*. Aware that pan-Islamist ideas would not offer much appeal to the many Hindu and Sikh POWs, the members of the IIC who were involved with the production of the paper suggested the title *Hindostan* for the Hindi and Urdu editions of the newspaper.[46] To cater to the different religious segments of the Indian POW population, the tenor of the two editions of the papers varied as well. This difference was visible on the masthead of the different editions itself. While the Hindi edition contained two slogans, Bankim Chandra's *Bande Mataram* and Iqbal's *Sare jahan se accha Hindostan hamara*, the Urdu version only referred to Iqbal's words. Even in content there were occasional differences that indicated an awareness that different sentiments of different audiences needed to be appealed to. For example, a story about Id ul-Fitr and the opening of the mosque in the Halfmoon Camp was published on the first page of the Urdu edition of the paper, but the Hindi edition published an appeal to the sepoys to fight for the *svatantrata* (freedom) of India and not for the British.[47] The papers were also notable for addressing topics of political and economic developments that were taking place across the world. The developments in Russia after the communist revolution received coverage. More patriotic topics such as Britain's economic exploitation of India and the unfairness of the tax system were discussed alongside issues of a more historical nature, such as the 1857 mutiny. '*Hindustan men teks ka zulm*' (The tyranny of tax in India) noted one headline while the article on 1857 stated '*Angrezon ka zulm mat bhulo. Ab badla lene ka samay aa gaya he*' (Do not forget the tyranny of the British. The time for taking revenge has come).[48]

The German authorities did have some success in getting volunteers for their attempts to stir up rebellion in India. Some soldiers perhaps believed in the German cause; others might have been purporting to be fervent because doing so would give them a chance of passage back to India. In July 1915, the *New York Times* published an article noting that some hundred Indian troops had escaped from Constantinople and were making their way back to India, pointing to the opportunities to make it back home the landscape of the war offered some Indians at least.[49] However, this course of action was perhaps more viable for those who lived on the Indo-Afghan border where British authority was not as pervasive.[50] For most of the Gurkhas, Sikhs and Punjabi Muslims, fighting for Turkey was out of the question as they and their families depended on the British for pay, pension, and social status. Moreover, the German enthusiasm for Holy War might also have impacted the ability to harness any appeal anti-colonial revolution might have had. Perhaps acutely aware that they would only be trading imperial masters some Hindu soldiers expressly stated that while they were willing to fight for India, they did not want to take up arms for Turkey or Germany.[51]

By the spring of 1916 the notion of deploying Indian POWs for military purposes against the British had been abandoned. Once military propaganda in the camps had lost its significance, they were approved as sites for anthropological and ethnographic research. German anthropologists, linguists, and musicologists had recognized the opportunity this presented for their disciplines. In many ways, it is this brief life span of the camps as sites of ethno-linguistic research that provides us with the clearest sense of the isolation and despair the war caused for many of these soldiers.

On 14 December 1916, the sepoy Mall Singh committed the following words to a shellac disk:

> There once was a man.
> He ate one ser of butter every day in India.
> He drank two ser of milk every day in India.
> He joined the British Army.
> This man came to the European war.
> Germany captured this man.
> He wishes to go back to India.
> When he returns, he will get the same food as in former times.
> Three long years have passed.
> Nobody knows when there will be peace.
> In case this man is forced to stay here for another two years – he will surely die.
> If God has mercy, this man will return home soon.[52]

Located about fifty miles outside Berlin in the former East German town of Wünsdorf is a forgotten cemetery that marks the site where 206 First World War POWs from India are buried. The cemetery, now maintained by the Commonwealth War Graves Commission, was re-inaugurated in 2007 after decades of ruin and neglect as a result of its location in a forbidden Soviet military zone. Like the voices of the *Lautarchiv*, the neat white gravestones at the cemetery act as a reminder that there were indeed Indian POWs in these lands. There is, however, no record of Mall Singh in the Wünsdorf cemetery. Perhaps he did return home.

+++

Religious Imagery in a Time of War

Do not think that this is war. This is not war. It is the ending of the world. This is just such a war as was related in the Mahabharata about our forefathers.

– A wounded Punjabi Rajput soldier to a relative

Religion was never far from the war experience for most serving Indians. Unsurprisingly, religious rites became a way for the troops to cling on to a sense of order and normality at a time of war. For most Indian soldiers who found themselves in the midst of the war, it was a challenge to make sense of the surreal and unreal nature of the war they found themselves in. The war was not just being fought in a completely unfamiliar environment, but the industrialized methods of warfare were quite new for a majority of those who found themselves on the frontline. The troops often relied on familiar imagery to make the bizarre and calamitous circumstances they found themselves in accessible and understandable. Classical religious themes were a common occurrence in their letters with soldiers of all religious denominations referring to epics and stories to tell their stories.

For Hindu soldiers the most common reference was the Mahabharata, the great Hindu epic whose central plot line is a brutal familial war. This war like the one in the epic not only had unimaginable weapons, but was also a family affair. As one soldier plainly noted, 'so what if the German and British kings were brothers (they were both grandsons of Queen Victoria), so were the Kauravas and Pandavas in the Mahabharata and they too had embarked on a bloody, all-consuming war'.

Amar Singh Rawat, a rifleman from the Garhwal Rifles brought the battle scenes at Neuve Chapelle vividly to life in their entire epic and futile glory for a friend back home:

> The condition of affairs in the war is like leaves falling off a tree, and no empty space remains on the ground. So it is here: the earth is full of dead men and not a

A painting by an Indian POW of Lord Ganesh.

> vacant spot is left. One has to stay on top of the corpses and even sleep on them, because not an empty space remains anywhere. Such is the scene that goes on here. You have heard the war between the Kauris and the Pandevs was a great conflict, but it was not so great a fight as this one. When we attacked the German trenches we used the bayonet and the kukri, and the bullets flew about more thickly than drops of rain. Consider this true: there was not an empty spot on the ground. In some places men had lost their eyes, in others men [were] without legs, but what could one do? As is one's fate, so it will happen. Such is the scene and one was powerless. Now I have not any sure confidence that I will see you people again; there is nothing but hopelessness.

The parallel with the most devastating of all conflicts was also drawn to remove any naïve notions that friends and family might have about the war as some sort of great adventure. Trying to dissuade a friend back in India for signing up for war, a Sikh soldier wrote:

> You proposed to enlist and come to France. You are lucky because you did not. Perhaps someone may escape from this war. On the 10th, 11th and 12th the Meerut Division made an attack and won a great victory. We took three trenches, wounded 600 and killed 400. A splinter of shell hit me. I am well again. The German guns throw a shell, which digs a hole in the ground 35 feet wide and 114 feet deep. My brother such a war will not be again, nor such a war has been before. It is Mahabharata, the death of the Punjaub.

Muslim soldiers too relied heavily on Islamic imagery to describe the war. For them this was 'not [ordinary] fighting, it is Karbala'. This battle where Husayn ibn Ali, the grandson of the Prophet was defeated and killed was an apt metaphor for the soldiers to draw on. Abdul Ghani, a Punjabi Muslim sepoy, wrote a deeply moving letter rich in Islamic imagery to his brother from the frontlines in France, referencing not just Karbala, but also the story of Ishmael:

> My friend, to us travellers the time passes as it did at Karbala when our high priest [Husayn, the younger son of Ali] fought and met his death as a martyr at the hand of the infidels. Then our warriors used to meet in the morning and march off, saying to one another "farewell: go, and God be with thee". So they died the death of martyrs. In like manner the time passes with us, who with our brothers and relatives, have men in thousands, and remain congregated together, and seated writing until the lives quit the bodies of those whose time has come…
>
> See our prophets who gave their sons in the way of God. When the Almighty by way of trial ordered Abraham (on whom be peace!) to sacrifice his son Ishmael he was pleased and said: "Amen; for thou O God gavest him to me, and he is thy property." And when Abraham took his son, his beloved son, into the wilderness to sacrifice him, he said to him "my son! I am about to sacrifice you in the name of God." Then Ishmael also was pleased and said "Oh my father! Bind my hands and my feet with cords; that way, when you slay my body, neither my hands nor my feet shall be in your way; for my will is His will."
>
> My brother, you should give thanks to God, and remember me, your poor brother, for my time is come to be sacrificed. At some time the knife of death will descend. Pray God may be gracious both in this world and the next, for His mercy is necessary.

If some soldiers turned to religion in fatalist despair, for others religious and military duty combined to spur them on to action. Such was the case with Subedar Narain Singh of the 14th Sikhs who received six bullet wounds while engaged in action in Gallipoli. Singh claimed that the vision of Guru Gobind Singh appeared before the Sikh soldiers just as they brandished their bayonets. For Singh, 'the spirit this holy sight infused in us… emboldened us to march on, piercing thorough the abdomen of the enemy. We shouted Sat Sri Akal – the battle cry of the Sikhs – and chanted shabads of halla (attack)… the only thought before us was devotion to the Guru, who was omnipresent.'

A Muslim Indian soldier ritually washes his feet before praying as a German sentry observes him at the POW camp in Wünsdorf. The large Muslim population of the British Empire was seen to be its Achilles Heel by Germany. Muslim POWs in Germany were kept in the so-called Halfmoon Camp and winning over the Indian Muslim POWs was a stated objective of German policy during the war years.

सारे जहां से अच्छा हिन्दोस्तां हमारा ॥

हम बुल्बुलें हैं उसकी वह गुलिस्तां हमारा ॥

हिन्दोस्तान

बन्दे मातरम

अखबार हिन्दोस्तानी कैदियों के लिये जो अपने दोस्त जर्मनी के साथ लड़ाई के लिये भेजे गये हैं ॥

परचा नः ९ | जर्मनी के पायातख़्त बरलीन से छपा | १४ जुलाई १९१५

Berlin den 14. Juli 1915

HINDOSTAN

Zeitung für die indischen Kriegsgefangenen

Nr. 9

Indische Ausgabe in Hindi

हिन्दुस्तान के सिपाहियो

हे हिन्दुस्तानी सिपाहियो तुम अपने देश की भलाई के विरुद्ध लड़ रहे हो और अपने हाथो को गुलामी की जञ्जीरो से जकड़ रहे हो। तुम शत्रुओं के लिये अपनी जान दे रहे हो और इस प्रकार अपने आप को नीच बना रहे हो। याद तो करो के तुम्हारे बाप दादा ने १८५८ में क्या किया था। मंगल पाण्डे, नाना साहिब रानी लक्ष्मी बाई, कमार सिंह, अज़ीम उल्ला खान तान्तया तोपी, मौलवी अहमद शाह और गदर के और बड़े बहादरों के नाम याद करो। १८५६ में हिन्दी सिपाही अच्छी तरह समझ गये थे कि अंग्रेजों ने उन को नीच बना दिया है। वह जान गये थे कि अंग्रेज हिन्दुस्तान के धोकेबाज़ और सख़्त दुशमन हैं। उन को यह विदित हो गया था कि प्रतयेक जाति जरूर स्वतन्त्रता होनी चाहिये इसी कारण वह सवतन्त्रता के लिये सूरबीरों की तरह लड़े थे। और मरते समय उन को यह आशा थी कि उन की सन्तान स्वतन्त्रता का झण्डा खड़ा करेगी, और तब तक युद्ध करेगी जब तक कि हिन्दुस्तान हिमालया से लेकर रास कुमारी तक आज़ाद न हो जाए।

वह सूझो स्वधर्म और स्वराज के अर्थें को अच्छी तरह जान्ते थे। भारतमाता की आवाज सुन कर वह उठ खड़े हुए। लड़े और मर गये कियोंकि वह समझ गये थे कि गुलाम रहने से मरना अच्छा है। हिन्दी सिपाहियो तुम आज अंग्रेज़ो की नौकरी कर रहे हो। उन बहादरों की आत्माऐं तुम से पूछती हैं "क्या हमारा मरना बेफ़ाइदा था"। तुम उन की सन्तान हो और उन की लकीर पर चलते हो। तुम्हें इस बात का फैसला करना चाहिये। क्या तुम आज़ादी के लिये युद्ध करना चाहते हो या गुलाम रहना। और शत्रुओं के वास्ते लड़ना चाहते हो। तुम्हारा देश इस सवाल का उत्तर मांगता है। लाखों मरद औरतें, तम्हारे भाई और बच्चे भूके मर रहे हैं और तम से पूछते हैं। क्या तुम अपने देश को आज़ाद करोगे या सदा गुलाम बने रहोगे जिन की किसमत में हमेशा फिटकार ही लिखी है।

हिन्दी सिपाहियो तुमहारे देश की उन्नति तुम्हारे हाथ में है। भारतमाता आशा करती है कि तुम स्वतन्त्रता के लिये युद्ध करोगे और उस की गुलामी की ज़ञ्जीर तोड़दोगे याद रखो कि जर्मन तुम्हारे शत्रू नहीं हैं। अंग्रेज़ तम्हारे शत्रू हैं जिनहों ने तुमको अपने अधीन किया हुवा है, वह तुम को मारते पीटते हैं। तुमहारी स्त्रियो का अपमान करते हैं। तुम्हारे मन्दिर और मसजिदें अपवित्र करते हैं और तुम को हिकारत की आंख से देखते हैं। अब सोचो कि अपना राज होने का

यह समय है। गुलामी की जन्जीर तोड़ने का यही समय है। अपने भाईयों को आज़ाद करवाने का यही समय है। यह समय जाओ और स्वतन्त्रता का युद्ध शुरु कर दो। तलवार हाथ में लेकर तुम जर्मनों के विरुद्ध क्यों लड़ते हो, वह तो तुम्हारे मित्र हैं यह शस्त्र अंग्रेज़ों पर चलाओ और अपने देश को आज़ाद करो। तुमहारी भारत माता तुम को आशीर्वाद देगी और सारा जगत तुम्हारा आदर करेगा।

दुन्या तुम से पूछती है क्या तुम इतने भोले हो कि तुम शत्रुओ के लिये जान देते हो। क्या तुम माशा भर भी देश भक्त नहीं कि तुम इस समय जब कि सारा संसार युद्ध में फंसा हुआ है अपने देश को आज़ाद नहीं करते।

हिन्दी सिपाहियो। यही समय है आज़ादी के लिये सर उठाने का। यह मत भूलो कि परमात्मा केवल उन की सहायता करता है। जो अपनी सहायता आप करते हैं। कोई अवतार या महदी तुम्हारी मदद करने के लिये आकाश से नहीं उतरेगा। यदी तुम स्वय उद्यम न करोगे। अवतार और महदी तुम्हारे बीच होंगे। जब तुम सवतन्त्रता के लिये युद्ध करोगे। इस समय जर्मन लोग अंग्रेज़ों की खूब खबर ले रहे हैं। सैवन उन का पराजय कर रहे हैं टरकी के सुलतान ने अंग्रेज़ों के विरुद्ध युद्ध का घोषन कर दिया है। और शेख़ उल इसलाम ने हिन्दुस्तान के मुसलमानों को हिन्दुओ के साथ मिल जाने का फतवा दिया है और अंग्रेज़ों को हिन्दुस्तान से निकाल दो, इस कारण हिन्दी सिपाहियो अंग्रेज़ों के वास्ते ना लड़ो। परन्तु आज़ादी के लिये। यही समय है भारत माता को स्वतन्त्र करने का

१९१०,००० कैदी

१४ जून तक जर्मनी और आस्टरिया की फौज़ों ने इतने कैदी बनाये थे,

रूसी	१२४०,०००
फ्रांसीसी	२५५,०००
अंग्रेज़	२४,०००
बैलगयर	४२,०००
सर्बियन	५०,०००
कुल	१९१०,०००

इन दिनों गालीसिया की फतह के कारण इनकी संख्या बहुत बढ़ गई है

हिन्दुस्तान में बे चैनी

"मौर्निंग पोस्ट" अखबार कलकत्ते से यह खबर देता है: पन्जाब में अमरितसर के ज़िले में बड़ी बेचैनी फैली हुई है। नहर का पुल पर पहरा अंग्रेज़ों लगा हुआ था। हिन्दी उन पर आ पड़े और उन को मार डाला बहुत से लोग ज़ख्मी हुवे। अमरितसर वह ज़िला है। जहां ग़दर का काम हो रहा है। पन्जाब में अंग्रेज़ों के विरुद्ध बड़ी साज़शें हो रही हैं। कचहरी ने चन्द लोगों पर बड़े सख्त हुक्म पास किये हैं। यह हम को हिन्दुस्तान के अंग्रेज़ी अखबारों के द्वारा विदित हुआ है। सानफ्रांसिसको अमरीका में एक हिन्दी सौदागर पहुंचा है उस ने अमरीका के पत्रलेखों को कहा है कि हिन्दुस्तान में इस समय अवस्था बड़ी नाज़ुक है। अंग्रेज़ बड़े खबरदार हैं। वह खबरें बाहिर जाने नहीं देते।

रयूटर कलकत्ते से खबर देता है कि गौर्मिंट ने बकरगंज में जो गंगा के दहाने पर है जंगी कानून चला दिया है। १०० आदमी पकड़े गये हैं। दो अफ़गानी शाहज़ादे सीमा की और बिना इजाज़त लिये लाहौर से भाग गये थे। अंग्रेज़ उन को पकड़ कर फिर लाहौर ले आए हैं।

अंग्रेज़ बड़े यत्न करते हैं कि हिन्दुस्तान से खबरें बाहिर न जाऐं। परन्तु सच्चाई एक न एक दिन मालूम हो ही जाती है। अंग्रेज़ी राज हिन्दुस्तान से ज़रूर जलदी ही चल देगा॥

سارے جہاں سے اچھا ہندوستان ہمارا

ہم بلبلیں ہیں اسکی وہ گلستان ہمارا

ہندوستان

اخبار ہندوستانی قیدیوں کیلئے جو اپنے دوست جرمنی کے خلاف لڑائی کیلئے بھیجے گئے ہیں

جرمنی کے پایہ تخت برلین سے چھپا

پرچہ نمبر ۲

۹ اپریل سنہ ۱۹۱۵ء

Berlin
den 9. April 1915

HINDOSTAN
Zeitung für die indischen Kriegsgefangenen

Nr. 2
Indische Ausgabe in Urdu

جہاد

تم جانتے ہو کہ جرمنی کے دشمن اسلام کے بھی دشمن ہیں۔ فرانس و انگلستان اور روس نے عہد کیا ہے کہ حضرت محمدؐ کے پیروکاروں کو غلام بنا دیں اور انکا خانہ خراب کر دیں۔ اسی وجہ سے حضرت کے جانشین سلطانِ روم نے جہاد کا اعلان دیا اور تمام مسلمانوں کو حکم دیا کہ دشمنانِ اسلام سے جنگ کریں۔ تمہارے ظالم حکمرانوں نے بہت کوشش کی کہ کسی طرح سے تمکو اس اعلان کی اطلاع نہ ہو کیونکہ انکو اندیشہ تھا کہ تم پھر اپنا ہو فوجِ اسلام کے دشمنوں کے واسطے لڑنے سے انکار کر دوگے لیکن اس وقت تم اپنے ظالموں سے جدا ہو اس وجہ سے مناسب ہے کہ تمکو جہادِ شریف کے اسباب اور مضمون سے پوری پوری طرح مطلع کیا جاوے +

سال گذشتہ کی ۱۴ نومبر کو شیخ الاسلام نے استنبول کے شہر میں فتیح مسجد پر بیس ہزار دینداروں کی موجودگی میں جنگ جہاد کا اعلان دیا جو بصورت سوال شیخ الاسلام کے پاس پیش کیا گیا تھا۔ فتوے کا مضمون حسب ذیل ہے

"جب بہت سے دشمنانِ اسلام اتفاق کریں۔ جب مسلمانوں کے ملک تباہ و غارت کئے جاویں جب مسلمان لوگوں پر ظلم کیا جاوے اور انکو قید کیا جاوے اور جب اس صورت میں شاہِ اسلام بموجب آیت شریف قرانِ مبارک جہاد کا اعلان دیوے تو یہ لڑائی سب مسلمانوں پر لازمی ہے خواہ وہ بوڑھے ہوں یا جوان۔ پیدل ہوں یا سوار اور یہ بھی لازم ہے کہ تمام مسلمانی ملک جہاد شروع کر دیں اور جوش سے مال و جان اس پر قربان کریں + جواب۔ بیشک + سلطان روس۔ فرانس۔ انگلستان اور دوسرے بادشاہوں کی بھی رعایا ہیں جو خلیفۂ اسلام پر بذریعہ جہاز اور زمینی فوج حملہ آور ہیں۔ اور اسلام کے غارتگیری کرتی ہیں۔ تو کیا ان مسلمانوں پر بھی واجب ہے۔ کہ وہ اپنے حکمرانوں کے برخلاف جہاد میں شامل ہوں جواب۔ بیشک + وہ لوگ جو کسی موقعہ پر باوجود جہاد کے اعلان کے جہاد نہیں کرتے اور اسمیں شریک ہونے سے معترض ہیں تو کیا اُن پر عذابِ خدا نازل ہوگا اور کیا وہ گناہ کے موجب ہیں اور کیا اُنکو سزا ملیگی جواب بیشک + مسلمان مذکورہ یالاسلا طین کی رعایا ہیں جنہوں نے کہ اسلام کے برخلاف جنگ آغاز کی ہے تو کیا یہ مسلمان سخت گناہگار نہیں اگر وہ اپنی جان و مال اور اپنے تمام خاندان کی زندگی سے خوف کھا کر اسلام کے برخلاف جنگ کرتے ہیں۔ جواب۔ بیشک + مسلمان جنگ حال میں انگلستان۔ فرانس۔ روس۔ سربیا۔ مانٹی نگرو اور اُن سلاطین کی رعایا ہیں جو جرمنی اور آسٹریا ہنگری کے برخلاف دشمنوں کی مدد کرتے ہیں۔ تو کیا مسلمان عذابِ خدا کے مستحق ہیں جب وہ جرمنی آسٹریا ہنگری کے برخلاف جنگ کرتے ہیں کیونکہ جرمنی آسٹریا و ہنگری سلطان روم کے مددگار ہیں اور جرمنی آسٹریا و ہنگری کے برخلاف جنگ کرنے سے حضرت سلطان روم کو نقصان پہنچتا ہے جواب۔ بیشک + دینداروں کے انبوہ کثیر نے اس فتوے کے مضمون کو لاانتہا جوش سے سنا۔ انہوں نے سلطان روم کے دارالسلطنت کے بازاروں میں خوشی کے جلوس نکالے۔ اور وکیل جرمن کے مکان کے سامنے جو اسلام کا دوست ہے۔ محبت سے اور بھی لائے۔ تم کو اس موقعہ کی کیفیت سننے سے بہت لطف آویگا جبکہ باشندگانِ اسلام وکیل جرمن سے ملے۔ وکلا کے بازار کے مقابل نعیل پرتی سیون۔ الجیریوں اور مراکو کے مسلمانوں کے قاصد بیٹھے تھے۔ یہ لوگ فرانس میں اہلِ جرمن کے ہاتھ لگے تھے۔ اور اسی وجہ سے جرمنی میں قید تھے حضور قیصر جرمنی نے پھر ان لوگوں کو رہا کر دیا۔ اس سے ثابت ہے۔ کہ حضور مسلمانوں کے کیسے اعلےٰ دوست ہیں یہ لوگ سلطان روم کے سپرد کر دئے گئے۔ اور چند روز پیشتر ہی شہر استنبول میں وارد ہوئے تھے۔ ان قاصدوں کے رہبر نے پھر ایک موثر تقریر کی جسکو ہزاروں مسلمانوں نے سنا۔ اسمیں اسنے بیان کیا۔ کہ جرمنی اسلام کی دوست ہے۔ اور انگلستان۔ فرانس۔ روس سخت دشمن ہیں۔ اس تقریر میں اسنے یہ بھی کہا کہ فرانس مسلمانوں کو اُن کی رضا کے برخلاف میدانِ جنگ میں بھیج رہا ہے۔ اور سپاہیوں سب اگلی قطاروں میں کھڑے کئے جاتے ہیں جہاں وہ توپ اور گولہ کی خوراک بنتے ہیں۔ اس شخص نے ذاتی تجربہ سے یہ سب معلومات کی تھیں۔ اور اس کی تقریر کا اثر حاضرین پر بہت پڑا۔ اور پھر انہوں نے اپنے آزاد شدہ برادران کو بہت خوشی سے بغلگیر کیا۔ اور بعد ازاں سلطنت جرمنی کے واسطے نعرے بلند کئے۔ جو مسلمانوں کی دوست اور پشت و پناہ ہے۔ پھر حضرت سلطان نے جو خلیفہ اسلام ہیں۔ حضرت محمدؐ کے جبہ کے روبرو ٹروپ کاپو کے سرائیل میں ان لوگوں کے قاصدوں کا استقبال کیا۔ اور اس موقعہ پر دینی و دنیاوی سردار موجود تھے۔ سلطان نے بھی قوم عثمانیہ اور تمام دنیا کے مسلمانوں کو اعلان دیا۔ جس میں ان حضرت نے اس جنگ کے تمام اصلی اسباب بتائے۔ اور تمام دینداروں کو بتلایا۔ کہ ان کا اس کشمکش میں کیا حصہ ہے۔ یہ علاج تمام مسلمانوں کے لئے ضروری ہے۔ اگلے اخبار میں اسکو شائع کرینگے + دینی جنگ کا بھی اعلان دیا گیا۔ آزادی کا موقع آگیا تھا۔ دنیا کے مسلمانوں کا دل جوش سے پُر تھا۔ دینی لڑائی کا یہ جوش سلطان روم کے دارالخلافہ سے شروع ہوا۔ اور پھر تمام ملکوں میں پھیل گیا۔ جہاں کہ حضرت محمدؐ کے دیندار بستے ہیں۔ اس فتوے کی تحریر کے موجب اور اپنے دینی فرائض کے مطابق مسلمان اپنے دینی مذہب کے واسطے مصروف ہو گئے۔ عثمانی بہادر فوج انگلستان کے برخلاف فتحیاب ہوئی اور نہر سویز تک جا پہنچی۔ اور روس میں کوہ قاف تک۔ مراکو میں دیندار فرانسیسی ظلم کے برخلاف اُٹھے۔ فارس۔ افغانستان۔ اور ہندوستان میں بھی جہاد کا زور بڑھ گیا۔ مسلمانوں میں کبھی ایسا اتفاق نہیں ہوا۔ اور انکی طاقت کبھی اس عروج پر نہیں پہنچی۔ جیسے کہ آج ہے۔ مسلمانوں کے دشمن کبھی آج تک ایسے خوفزدہ نہیں ہوئے۔ جیسے کہ آج ۳۰ کروڑ دینداروں کے مقابلے میں + خوش قسمتی سے آج ایک موقع ہے کہ تم بھی اسمیں شامل ہو سکتے ہو۔ تمہارے دیندار برادر ایشیا میں جانتے ہیں۔ کہ وہ کس مدعا سے جنگ کر رہے ہیں۔ وہ لڑتے ہیں۔ اپنے یقینی پاک مذہب کیواسطے۔ اپنے ملک کی آزادی کیواسطے۔ اپنے بچوں اور اپنے بیوی کی خوشحالی اور بہتری کیواسطے۔

تم کسواسطے اپنا خون بہاتے ہو۔ انگلستان، فرانس و روس کے ظلم نے تمکو مجبور کیا ہے۔ اور تم اپنے جفاکار حکمرانوں

کیطرف ہوکر اپنے دوستوں یعنی اپنے آپ کے برخلاف لڑو۔ خدا کی لعنت اُن کافروں پر - اونہوں نے تمکو اپنے مذہب کے پاک فرائض ادا کرنے سے روکا ہے - اور وہ فرض یہ ہے کہ تم سب حضرت نبی کے جھنڈے کے نیچے جمع ہو - جب تم بعد میں اپنے ملک واپس جاؤگے - تو تمکو موقع ہوگا - کہ تم اپنے آپ کو اِس گناہ سے صاف کرو - اِسکا ذریعہ صرف یہ ہے - کہ تم اپنے برادران میں اِس اطلاع کو خوب شایع اور مشتہر کر دو + انکو آزادی کی خوشخبری سناؤ - اور وہ جب تک غیر قوموں کے ماتحت ہوں - انکی آنکھیں کھولو اور انکو جگا دو - تاکہ وہ غلامی کے طوق کو دور کر دیں - صرف اسی صورت میں تم فتوے کے مطابق عمل درآمد کروگے اور اسی صورت میں دشمنانِ اسلام کے برخلاف اپنے پاک مذہب کے مطابق فتوے شریف کے ثواب میں حصہ دار ہوگے -

جرمنی کی نئی فتح

ہنڈنبرگ کی لاانتہا لوٹ فتح کے بعد

ایک لاکھ سے زیادہ روسی قیدی

جرمن فوجی سردار تحریر کرتا ہے - ماسوریا میں سرما کی لڑائی کا اختتام ہوگیا - ہنڈنبرگ کے جنگی کے پاس جو گروڈونو کے شمال مغرب میں واقع ہے - اور بھور کی جنگ کے بعد جسکی خبر حال میں شایع کی جاچکی ہے اور نارو کے قرب و جوار میں مفصلہ ذیل مال و قیدی حاصل کیے گئے ہیں - ایک کمانڈر جنرل - دو ڈویژن کمانڈر اور دیگر جنرل - چالیس ہزار کے قریب سپاہی قیدی - 75 توپیں - ایک بڑی تعداد چھوٹی توپوں کی جو ابھی تک درست نہیں بتائی جاسکتی - اور دیگر سامان حرب (ابتک جو مال حاصل ہوا ہے) اجاڑنے کی لڑائی کے بعد اسکی کیفیت یہ ہے

گیارہ جنرل

ایک لاکھ سے زیادہ قیدی سپاہی

150 توپیں -

اور دیگر چھوٹی توپیں جنکی درست تعداد ابھی تک نہیں بتائی جاسکتی - جب ہمارے دشمن میدان سے بھاگے - تو انہوں نے اتواپ کلاں اور سامان حرب کو دفن کر دیا - یا پانی میں غرق کر دیا -

روسیوں کی فوج نمبر 10 جو جنرل باروں سیورس کے ماتحت تھی بالکل غارت ہوگئی - اِس نئی فتح کی خبر سے تمام جرمن سلطنت، آسٹریا و روم میں بے حد خوشی منائی جارہی ہے - نیوٹرل ممالک اظہارِ حیرت کرتے ہیں - کہ جرمن فوج نے کیسی بہادری کا کام کیا ہے - کہ اپنے دشمن کی کثیر التعداد کو شکست دیدی - خود دشمنوں نے بھی آہستہ آہستہ یہ سمجھنا شروع کر دیا ہے - کہ روسی فوج لڑائی میں ہمیشہ نتیجہ پائیگی - جرمن فوج کے برخلاف اپنے آپکو پورا غارت کریگی -

انگریزی ظلم کے برخلاف ہندوستان میں بغاوت -

ہندوستان میں بے چینی

جہان اسلام ایک اخبار ہے - جو شہر قسطنطنیہ سے ہندوستانی زبان میں شایع ہوتا ہے - اِس اخبار میں چند اخباریں تمہارے گھر ہندوستان سے آئی ہیں - اِنسے صاف معلوم ہوتا ہے - کہ تمہارے ملک کی حالت خراب ہے اور انگریزوں کے ظلم عوام الناس میں روز بروز ترقی پر ہے -

راجپوتوں کی رجمنٹ نمبر 8 ہانگ کانگ میں تھی - اسکو حکم دیا گیا - کہ یورپ جاوے - لیکن رجمنٹ نے انگریزوں کے واسطے لڑنے سے صاف انکار کر دیا - لہذا اسی رجمنٹ کو ہندوستان واپس جانا پڑا - لیکن راستہ میں جہاز ٹوٹ گیا - اور غرق ہوگیا - تمام ہندوستانی سپاہی ڈوب گئے + انگریزوں نے کہا - کہ جنہوں نے جہاز کو ڈبو دیا - لیکن تم خود سمجھ سکتے ہو - کہ اصلی واقعہ کیا ہے - انگریز ہر طرح سے کوشش کرتے ہیں - کہ ہندوستانی انگریزوں کے بیان کردہ اسباب جنگ پر یقین کریں - کیونکہ انگریز خوب سمجھتے ہیں - کہ ہندوستان کی مدد کے بغیر انگلستان جرمنی کا مقابلہ نہیں کرسکتا - یہ امر کہ ہندوستانی انگریزوں پر باور نہیں کرتے - اس سے ظاہر ہے - کہ ایک روز کلکتہ میں ہندوستانیوں نے اس شخص کو خوب مارا - جو انگریزوں کے واسطے بازاروں میں لڑائی کا چندہ جمع کر رہا تھا -

انمیں سے تین محب الوطن جو صرف اپنے ملک کے واسطے کام کر رہے تھے - گولی سے مار دئے گئے - آخر انگریزی پولیس اور باشندوں میں خوب لڑائی ہوئی - جسمیں انگریزی پولیس کے بہت سے نوجوان کام آئے -

ہندوستان کے بہت سے باشندوں میں غدر کے آثار روز بروز نمایاں ہوتے جاتے ہیں - پونا میں جہاں کہ ہندوستان کے مشہور باغی سردار مہاراج تلک رہتے ہیں - بہت سے آدمی گرفتار کئے گئے - اور انمیں سے بعض گولی سے مار دئے گئے - اور مقامات پر بھی بہت سے آدمی گرفتار ہوئے - اور انکا جرم صرف یہ تھا - کہ وہ اپنے ملک سے محبت کرتے تھے - الغرض انگریز ہر ظلم کے طریق سے کوشش کر رہے ہیں - کہ ہندوستانیوں کو آزادی کی بو نہ لگے لیکن باوجود اِس تمام سعی کے انگریزوں کے برخلاف نفرت روز بروز بڑھتی جاتی ہے - اور ایک روز ایک جنگ عظیم کی صورت میں نمودار ہوگی - اور اِس جنگ کے بعد ہندوستان کو آزادی اور انصاف ملیگا -

انگلستان کا کرّہ امرا اسلام کا دشمن ہے

انگلستان کے کرّہ امرا کے آخری اجلاس کے موقعہ پر صاف ثابت ہوگیا - کہ انکو اہل اسلام سے اسقدر نفرت ہو رہی ہے - کہ وہ کبھی دور نہیں ہوسکتی سلطنت ہند نے مسلمانوں کو ایکا وعدہ کیا تھا - کہ صوبہ متحدہ آگرہ و اودھ کو ایگزیکٹیو کونسل دی جاویگی - یہ ایک بہت چھوٹی سی بات تھی - لیکن مغرور انگریزی امرا نے اسکو بھی بہت بڑا امر سمجھا اور مظلوم مسلمانوں پر سختی روا رکھی - اگر ہندوستانی گورنمنٹ نے ایکا وعدہ کیا تھا - پھر بھی کرّہ امرا نے لارڈ میک ڈونلڈ کی نصیحت کے مطابق کونسل دینے سے صاف انکار کیا - انگریزی اخبار بھی اِس وحشیانہ طریقہ ظلم سے متنفر ہوگئے - اور وہ تحریر کرتے ہیں کہ اندیشہ ہے - کہ کرّہ امرا کے اِس فیصلہ سے سلطنت ہند کی طاقت کو نہایت نقصان پہنچیگا - اور یہ افسوسناک واقعہ اوسوقت پیش آیا - جبکہ سلطنت ہند ہر طرف سے مسلمانوں کی نمک حلالی کی شیخیاں بگھار رہی ہے -

یہ آخری فقرہ نہایت پر معنی ہے - اِس سے صاف ظاہر ہے - کہ انگریز اِس امر سے سخت بے چین ہیں - کہ جب ہزاروں مسلمان روز انکے واسطے خون بہا رہے ہیں - تو پھر اونکو غلام کیطرح برتنا نہایت شرم ہے - انگریزوں کو اندیشہ ہے - کہ آخر ایک روز آویگا - جب صابر سے صابر آدمی بھی بے چین ہوکر اُٹھ کھڑا ہوگا - اوسوقت تمام دشمنان اسلام خوفزدہ ہیں - یہ وقت وہ ہوگا - جب مسلمان غلامی اور ظلم سے آزاد ہو جاوینگے - اور اسقدر طاقت اور عروج حاصل کرینگے - کہ اپنے لاانتہا مسلمانی برادران کی مدد سے دشمنان اسلام کو تباہ و غارت کر دینگے - (کیا یہ انگریز اپنی مرضی سے مظلوم مسلمانوں کو آزادی کبھی دینگے اکثر امور کے اِس امر سے صاف ظاہر ہے) مسلمانوں کے پاس صرف ایک یہ چارہ ہے - کہ وہ آزادی کے واسطے اپنا خون بہائیں - اِن پر لازم ہے - کہ وہ اپنے ظالموں کو خاک سے ملادیں - اگر وہ یہ چاہتے ہیں - کہ آئندہ وہ اور انکے بچے خوش حالی سے زندگی بسر کریں -

مصر میں انگریزوں کی خوفناک حکومت +

قسطنطنیہ سے معتبر خبر آئی ہے - کہ مصر میں انگریزوں کی حالت روز بروز ابتر ہوتی جاتی ہے - ہندوستانی فوج انگریزی ظالموں کے واسطے اپنے دینی برادروں سے جنگ کرنے سے قطعی انکار کر دیا ہے - لاچار انگریزوں نے اِن فوجوں کو ہندوستان واپس بھیجدیا - صرف تین یا چار ہندوستانی پلٹنیں مصر میں ابھی تک ہیں - جو فوجیں کینیڈا و آسٹریلیا سے آئی ہیں - وہ قاہرہ اور اور محصور مقامات میں عیش کر رہی ہیں اِسی وجہ سے مصر میں انگریزوں سے نفرت و حقارت روز افزوں ترقی پر ہے - انگریزوں نے حسین کامل کو مصر کا بادشاہ مقرر کر دیا ہے - یہ امر انصاف کے بالکل برخلاف ہے -

حسین کامل برادری سے خارج ہے - کیونکہ اسکا چال چلن نہایت شرمناک ہے - لوگ اسکی بے عزتی کرتے ہیں - انہوں نے اِس امر کی بھی کوشش کی - کہ کیطرح اِس ناپاک کو قتل کیا جاوے - مسلمانوں میں تمام جوش پھیلا ہوا ہے - کہ انگریزوں نے اِس نالائق کو راج کی گدی پر متمکن کر دیا ہے - اور نماز کے وقت حسین کامل کا نام لیا جاتا ہے - تو دینی لوگ سب کے سب اللہ اللہ پکارتے ہیں +

Pages 172 to 175: To further its propaganda efforts amongst Indian POWs, the German Foreign Office published Hindi and Urdu editions of the camp newspaper, titled *Hindostan*. The tenor of the two editions of the papers varied to cater to the different religious segments of the Indian POW population. The mastheads of the papers encapsulated this variance. The Hindi edition contained two slogans, Bankim Chandra's *Bande Mataram* and Iqbal's *Sare jahan se accha Hindostan hamara*, the Urdu version only referenced Iqbal's words.

Facing page and above: A group of Afridi and Gurkha Indian POWs pose together at the POW camp in Wünsdorf.

Sikh soldiers taken prisoner by the Germans during the Battle of Neuve Chappelle (10–13 March 1915).

Sikh POWs photographed with and without their turbans.

The majority of photographs from German POW camps that survive today were taken by Otto Stiehl, the second in command of the Halfmoon Camp from June 1917. Stiehl had a passion for photography and took pictures in the camp throughout his time there in a personal capacity. The prisoners in the camp were subjects of great interest to Stiehl and a number of images in his collection are portraits of POWs. Pictured left to right are Abdullah Khan, an Afridi from Waziristan; Fazl Dad, a Punjabi; and an unidentified Gurkha soldier.

Left to right: Dingal Singh, a Sikh from Punjab and Seru Ganga Ram, a Gurkha from Dharmshala. The third soldier, not photographed by Stiehl, is only identified by the title 'Indian Mahomedan'.

Sarswoti
D. 1st April 1927

Facing page and above: Surviving in German archives are a handful of paintings made by Indian POWs. The images here show paintings of Saraswati, the Hindu goddess of learning, and Hanuman, the monkey-god from the Ramayana.

Above and facing page: Indian soldiers are photographed dressed-up for the celebration of religious festivals. For Hindu soldiers, the most important festivals celebrated at the camp were the spring festivals of Holi and Fagu Purnima. It is not clear what festival was being celebrated when these photographs were taken, but some sources mention Ram Navmi or Dussehra. The outfits of the three soldiers in the picture on the right, complete with bow and arrows, do seem to indicate that perhaps it was a festival associated with the Ramayana.

हिन्दीस्तान

Halbmond-Lager in Wünsdorf-Zo

Vor den Baracken
Halbmond-Lager in Wünsdorf-Zossen

Im September von der 11. Komp. Inf.-Reg. 55 gefangene Hindus

Facing page and above: Like the British, the Germans too used images and postcards to further their propaganda aims. Postcards printed during the war showed the everyday life of colonial POWs in Germany in the hope of conveying that Germany had the moral upper hand in how it treated its prisoners. The postcards showed prisoners lounging around in the POW camp and engaging in a variety of games and activities.

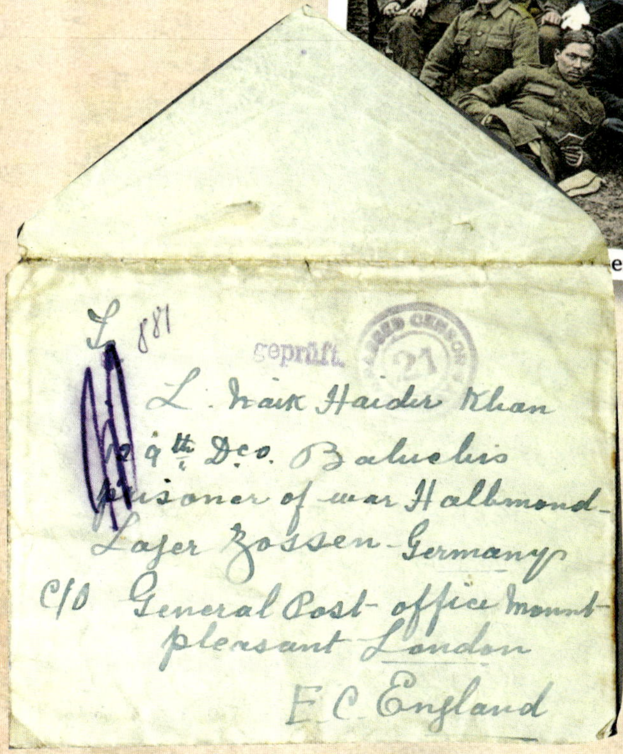

Above: A postcard shows the mosque built at the POW camp in Wünsdorf. The mosque held the distinction of being the first erected on German soil.

Left: An envelope addressed to a Lance Naik Haider Khan made its way to Zossen, though its contents are yet unknown.

Englische
Kriegsgefangenen-Sendung
An die
Inder
18 JUIN 1917
Kriegsgefangenenlager Halbmondlag.
Zossen
BROTSENDUNG
№
Bern, Hilfsstelle f. K.-G.
Deutschland

Above: Postcards show Indian POWs engaged in games (including a three-legged race) at the POW camp in Wünsdorf.

Left: A slip shows the details of a parcel for a POW in the camp.

343 Gefangenenlager Wünsdorf. Blick in die Indier-Baracke

378 Gefangenenlager Wünsdorf. Ein vergnügter Indier.

The image at the top shows the interiors of the barracks of Indian POWs at the Wünsdorf camp. Below, an Indian POW stands outside his quarters. These stereoscopic views, or stereographs, consist of two nearly-twin photographs – one for the left eye, and the other for the right. Viewing these side-by-side images through a special lens arrangement called a stereoscope, helps the brain combine the two flat images and 'see' the illusion of the objects in spatial depth. Such photography was most popular between 1850–1930.

Indian POWs are buried at a cemetery in the town of Wünsdorf. The cemetery was for decades unreachable due to its location in a forbidden Soviet military zone in East Germany. It was re-inaugurated in 2007 and is now maintained by the Commonwealth War Graves Commission.

An Indian sapper looks for a break in the cable that traverses the expanse of the barren Mesopotamian landscape. Mesopotamia was the Indian Army's most important front in terms of numbers of troops involved. It was also an immensely challenging place to wage war due to the precariousness of supply lines and the lack of infrastructure.

the Koran and prayers at the British lines in the hope of stopping the Muslim soldiers from fighting and causing desertions. During the siege of Kut, the Turks threw seditious pamphlets printed in Hindi and Urdu into the barbed wire of entrenchments during darkness, calling on the Muslim soldier not to fight against brothers of their own religion, offering lands and wives to those who deserted.

The Turks often adopted a full-fledged policy of favouritism towards Indian Muslim POWs. Though details of the Indian POW experience under the Turks are sketchy, there are accounts of captured Muslims being sent for the Hajj by the Ottoman authorities and being given tours of Istanbul and special audiences with Ottoman dignitaries. As in the case of German POW camps it was perhaps hoped that such fraternal solidarity and empathy would make the Indian POWs more receptive to propaganda and more likely to turn sides.

The British competed aggressively with Ottoman and German efforts at co-option, taking extra care to placate Muslim opinion within Indian battalions. Special precautions taken not to damage mosques, shrines or tombs during the fighting, especially in Mesopotamia where fighting was taking place close to sites such as Karbala and Salman Pak (the site of the tomb of Salman Farsi, a companion of Prophet Mohamed). On the Palestinian front, leave parties were organized to allow sepoys to see the religious sites. After the end of hostilities, small groups were taken from regiments for the pilgrimage to Mecca.

On balance, however, the British fears of a pan-Islamic revolution and the German belief that Islam would be the destruction of British India turned out to be highly exaggerated. Despite the few incidents of rebellion, Indian Muslim soldiers remained mostly steadfastly loyal. (The one notable exception were the Pathans whose desertion become problematic enough for the British to stop all recruitment of tans-frontier Pathans by the end of 1915. The Pathans probably deserted not simply for religious reasons, but also because the British did not formally govern their territories, thus making the bonds of patronage much weaker.) About the incident with the 15th Lancers at Basra, a Punjabi Muslim veterinary assistant wrote:

> When I read about the behaviour of the regiment I was overwhelmed by grief... This is the time to show loyalty and give help to the Government and not to be false to one's salt.

Perhaps the cultural differences within Islam were too great for it to act as unifying force for long. The Indian Army itself was representative of the various strains of Islam – Sunni, Shia but also the heterodox forms of subcontinental Islam – having recruited from Muslim communities from across India. The army recruited not just Punjabi Muslims (who made up nearly 20 per cent of the army) but also Pathans, rural Muslims from the Indo-Gangetic plain, Rajputana and the Central India and Deccani Muslims (who combined were almost 13 per cent of the army). It is not a stretch to suggest that not all of them would have had the same overarching religious concerns. If Indian Muslim soldiers remained loyal it was also because their individual concerns about loyalty, reward, progression and other such mundane matters were much more important than any sense of a larger Islamic *ummah*. As one Muslim officer wrote to his brother on Turkey's entry into the war:

> What better occasion can I find than this to prove the loyalty of my family to the British Government. Turkey, it is true, is a Muslim power, but what has it to do with us? Turkey is nothing at all to us.

the war would have to be fought. As a result, the underprepared troops and auxiliaries received a rude welcome to Mesopotamia. Abdul Rauf Khan, who was serving with the 21st Combined Field Ambulance in Mesopotamia, summed up the frustrations of dealing with the climate and terrain:

> The particular part of the world where I am is a strange place. The seasons here are quite different from what you experience anywhere else. We have already had experience of the cold and wet. Now the heat is threatening us from afar. It rains very heavily and the entire surface of the land becomes a quagmire in which the slush is knee deep. When I used to march in this slush, I used to remember God! Since I left India I have not seen a metalled road. Except for date trees which one sees here and there along the course of the river, there is not another tree to swear by. We drink river water. Wells cannot be dug here. Except for the barren, naked plain, there is nothing to see. The soil certainly is fertile, but the 'public' here are so thoughtless and careless that they do not make any attempt to till it. The lice infest one's clothes to such an extent that our hope [of release from them] is God alone. The summer is coming on gradually. It is stated here that the mosquitoes are enormous, and I have been afraid of them from the beginning.[10]

On reaching Basra, Captain Kalyan Mukherji, who was part of the 6th Ambulance Corps attached to the 6th Division wrote to his mother disparaging the town:

> *Arré* Ram! Can this be the Basra of Caliph Haroun al-Rashid? *Chhi, chhi!* There's not the faintest sign of the famous roses of Basra; instead there are shallow little creeks filled with knee- or waist-deep water from the Tigris. Every one of these khuds is home to hundreds of thousands of frogs. They come in all sizes, but most are big bullfrogs. What a fearsome roar they have! It's enough to deafen your ears. Men can't hear each other talk...[11]

Mesopotamia was to severely test the Indians who found themselves there. Between May and October temperatures could reach as high as 57 degrees C in the shade. Swarms of flies and locusts only made contending with the territory more difficult. It is telling that the British took to frequently referencing a purported Arab proverb: 'When Allah made Hell,' it went, 'he did not find it bad enough so he made Mesopotamia and added flies.' Winter brought no relief, bringing harsh weather with biting winds and bitter rains. The rain and desert were not friends; any significant downpour would turn the ground into a sea of glutinous mud, which made the movement of troops and animals almost impossible. Floods would turn the desert into stretches of impassable morasses.[12]

The desert was a difficult terrain to wage war in because of the lack of cover it afforded to the troops. In addition, there was the phenomenon of the mirage. Edmund Candler, a military journalist with the campaign noted that 'everything is magnified. A low-lying mud village become a fort with walls twenty feet high, a group of donkeys a palm grove... The first row of ducks I saw, I took for a battalion of infantry.'[13] The desert also posed difficulties of transport and logistics, as there were no real roads or railways. Supply was provided by traditional animal-drawn transport that was slow, inefficient, and limited by requirements of fodder and water.[14]

As a result, the two rivers that give Mesopotamia its name – '(land) between two rivers' – the Tigris and Euphrates became the main route for carriage of troops and equipment. But this too was a laborious and challenging process. From Basra, Baghdad could be reached by river craft but navigation was difficult, especially in the dry season when only small boats could make the journey, which in any case took at least five days.[15] This reliance on slow river transport severely impacted the army effort as it moved north from Basra towards Baghdad, as there was not enough river transport to supply the troops frequently. One of the most significant consequences was the lack of adequate rations. The dearth of fruits and vegetables, which had to be shipped from India and often spoiled by the time they reached the troops due to the lack of cold storage facilities, led to the appearance of scurvy amongst Indian soldiers as early as March 1915.[16] Malaria and cholera also became major concerns given the poor quality of water and the abundance of mosquitoes. On arriving in Mesopotamia one regimental medical officer noted 'we drink river water but it gives about half an inch of mud per tumbler'; another called it 'liquid mud'.[17]

The preventive measures adopted to mitigate the risks of cholera and malaria included the purification of water by boiling and chlorination, prophylactic dispensing of quinine, treatment of mosquito breeding places and the supply of mosquito nets. Photographs from the war show Indian troops lining up to receive dosages of quinine and the intricate steps taken to chlorinate and purify the water supply. Still, the water continued to be unsanitary.

Nor were there enough mosquito nets or fans to keep the insects at bay.[18] The cultural attitudes of some Indian troops compounded rather than aided these feeble attempts. In May 1915, half the regiment of the 27th Punjabis received its first inoculation against cholera. The tribal Khattacks in the regiment refused the inoculation because they believed this would render them impotent. They continued to refuse even when told that this inoculation was not voluntary but by order and had to be marched back to camp under arrest.[19]

These health challenges of operating in the desert coupled with the steady stream of battle wounded strained to breaking point the already poor medical infrastructure. Conditions here were a world away from the impromptu but efficient set-ups of the comparatively opulent hospitals in England. By contrast, in Mesopotamia IEFD was without a stationary hospital.[20] Not only was there a dearth of beds in the field ambulance sections, there was also a scarcity of vehicles to transport the wounded from the frontlines at times of military action.[21] As the campaign moved north from Basra the wounded had to be quickly evacuated on barges that had brought animals, men, and stores forward with no time allocated for cleaning.

As the troops began to press on towards Baghdad, the toxic mix of these conditions was to prove fatal for IEFD. The prolongation of IEFD's assignment began to impact the morale of the troops, especially as the enemy regrouped. In November 1915, the 6th (Poona) Division under the command General Charles Townshend made a push towards Baghdad from the town of Kut al-Amara. Within 30 kilometres of Baghdad, the force encountered strong Turkish positions at Ctesiphon, the site of the capital of the ancient Sassanian Empire. The Ottomans had received reinforcements of men and prepared their defenses well, forming a well-camouflaged and formidable line of trenches. The Ottoman force outnumbered the Indians. The battle that ensued was particularly bloody. Sisir Sarbadhikari who witnessed the confrontation as a stretcher-bearer nursing the wounded just behind the firing line recalled the scene in his memoirs:

> On all sides, the corpses of men and animals. In some places they seemed to be in each others' arms; in some places men had been pinned under animals and were lying there, groaning. In front of the trenches, along the lines of barbed wire, was where the greatest number of wounded lay. In some places men were hanging from the wires; some were dead (they were the lucky ones) and some were still alive. Here there was a severed hand hanging from the wire; there a foot. One man was hanging on the wires with all his entrails tumbling out. In some trenches four or five men had died with their limbs thrown over each other – Turkish, Hindustani, British, Gurkha, all mixed up together. One man's limb in another man's stomach, another's in someone's eye, that's how they were lying – and in the midst of this some were still alive – bringing them out was impossibly difficult ... I saw a Sikh sitting with a smile on his face – his white teeth were shining in his black beard. I thought, why are you smiling at a time like this, have you lost your head? When I approached I saw that he had been dead a while. He must have grimaced in pain as he was dying.[22]

Besieged

The loss at Ctesiphon was devastating. The heavy casualties (Townshend put the number at 4,300)[23] inflicted by the battle forced the Indian troops to turn around in a prolonged retreat with the Turks in hot pursuit. This was to be the road to a five-month-long siege, one of the most harrowing experiences for Indian troops anywhere during the war. The troops marched continuously for three days in hunger and cold. The desperation of their situations is brought to life by Sarbadhikari who wrote of an incident where he and another volunteer 'set off to look for food and found a piece of bread in the haversack of a dead white soldier. We divided it between us and were eating it in the dark, when we realized that the bread had a peculiar taste. Then we understood. The bread had soaked up the soldier's blood, hence the taste.'[24]

It was not just the lack of food that took its toll. At night the temperature would drop below freezing and the troops tried desperately not to sleep off for long periods at night for fear of frostbite. Having marched 44 miles in 36 hours with little water or food, they finally reached Kut. It was here that Townshend decided to make a stand, hopeful that reinforcements would soon arrive. Here his troops dug in, besieged, waiting in vain for a rescue before finally surrendering.[25]

For the most critically wounded, who had already endured a long, discomfiting journey to Kut, now began an almost 500-kilometre-long journey via river to Basra packed-to-the-rim in the few ships that were available. Major Carter of the Indian Medical Service who was waiting at Basra for the evacuated wounded described the arrival of one of the river convoys in what was to become the defining image of a campaign gone horribly wrong:

> The patients were so huddled and crowded together on the ship that they could not perform the offices of nature clear of the edge of the ship and the whole of the ship's side was covered with stalactites of human faece. ... we found a mass of men huddled up anyhow – some with blankets and some without... they were covered in dysentery and dejecta generally from head to foot.[26]

For the troops who remained garrisoned awaiting the arrival of a relief force life was hardly any better as they faced daily Turkish assaults. Sisir Sarbadhikari, who was billeted in a date orchard along with the rest of the Bengal Ambulance Corps, described the daily assaults from the enemy:

> One shell, instead of bursting above, hit a sepoy who was lying in bed, in one of the tents; it took off half his face before burying itself. The man rose to his feet as he was dying and then fell to the ground. His eyes, nose and mouth were all gone, there were only holes in his face, spouting blood. The sight was so ghastly that it created terror amongst the others in the tent.
>
> Through the whole day [the Turks] would bombard us; in the evening there would be rifle fire, an incessant whining of bullets. Not that there wasn't any machine-gunning rifle-volleys during the day. One morning I was sitting beside a young fellow called Anthony, of the I.G.H., drinking tea, when a bullet hit Anthony in the forehead. He died right there and his body fell on me. Another day a sepoy of the 7th Rajputs was sitting and chatting with us, when eight bullets hit him in the shoulder, just two or three inches apart.[27]

As the siege extended, the cold weather and accompanying rains became particularly taxing because of the dearth of blankets.[28] Moreover there was a shortage of clothes. The troops could not change or bathe. Everybody was covered with lice. 'They would swarm all over us, under our clothes. The torment was indescribable,' wrote Sarbadhikari.[29] By December, the morale of the troops was severely floundering. Several cases were reported of men shooting off their trigger fingers. The problem was troubling enough for adoption of preventive measures of the utmost severity – the death sentence.[30]

And yet, neither the cold nor the dismal medical conditions proved to be the most crucial problem during the siege. Instead, it was the increasing shortage of food that was to be an insurmountable obstacle. As the stock of vegetables dwindled and the garrison's fresh and tinned meat supplies were exhausted the force had to begin consuming its pack animals. This was a situation that posed particular problems for the Indians at Kut, many of whom refused to eat horse or mule, leaving them without an adequate source of protein.[31] Sensitive to the possibility of offending the Indians' religious sensibilities – again, concern that there would be a repeat of 1857 was paramount – Townshend obtained permission to quote the Imam of the Jama Masjid in Delhi and other 'leading' pundits and *granthis* that eating horsemeat was not objectionable. Still local consideration weighed on many Indian troops' minds. 'They declared that every village pundit would be against them on their return to India and that, in consequence, no one would give them their daughters to marry.'[32] This issue of horsemeat only worsened morale problems. Rather than break their caste, some preferred to commit suicide. To do this, they would walk to the riverbank, stand with folded arms, and wait for an enemy sniper to shoot them.[33] Others raised fears about loyalty by discouraging their comrades from eating horsemeat.[34]

Perhaps the expectation of an imminent rescue – which in the end did not reach in time – encouraged some of the troops' abstention from horsemeat. The Indian troops continued to subsist almost entirely on flour and unprocessed grain, which left them even more susceptible to scurvy and diseases such as pneumonia, jaundice and dysentery. This malnutrition further meant that the Indian troops became increasingly unable to recuperate from wounds and disease.[35] Health conditions became so bad that nearly twenty men were succumbing to disease each day. Photographs showing emaciated Indian soldiers, no more than mere bones and skin, hauntingly bring alive this period of starvation on the Indian soldiers.

Captain Kalyan Mukherji, who was one of the many Indians who spent the five long months at Kut under siege, poignantly wrote to his mother about the conditions he was faced with:

> Ma, it's been almost 5 months since I sat down to write to you. I've often thought of writing in these months but since nothing was known about when we would be able to send letters, I never got around to it. Since yesterday people here have come to accept that we will not be relieved. The troops have been on half-rations for the last month and even those have been steadily cut over the last 15 days, but despite these measures there's only enough food to last three more days.
>
> After three months with very little to eat the troops are starving. The mortality rate in the hospital has soared. In the last 15 days many have died for lack of food. Of what use is medicine now? There's nothing to eat. People are coming to the hospital because starvation has made them weak. With nothing to give them, how can we help? Apart from that, there are no medicines left either.
>
> The siege started on December 5th and it is now the 26th of April. But it's some consolation that things will be decided one way or another in the next 3 or 4 days and we will find ourselves either on this shore or that. We'll probably end up on the other shore. There's no way we could break out of the enemy's encirclement and rejoin our own side.[36]

Mukherji's fatalism about the impending end of the siege was sadly prophetic. At the end of April, with no help in sight, unable to offer his troops any more food Townshend surrendered, admitting to the Turkish Commander-in-Chief, Halil Paşa: 'Hunger forces me to lay down our arms ... I pray you to expedite the arrival of food.'[37]

Prisoners of the enemy

As the Indian Army reeled from the defeat at Kut and regrouped to launch another (ultimately successful) campaign to capture Baghdad those captured at Kut were living out another horrifying experience in their seemingly never-ending nightmare.

Writing to his family about the surrender at Kut, Karm Singh of the Sialkot Cavalry Brigade noted:

> It is a matter of very great regret that our brother Chet Singh has been taken prisoner at Kut al-Amara. ... Well, we should not grieve; nothing is to be gained by grieving. At the end of the war, they will return home alive.[38]

In fact, it is likely that Chet Singh never returned. Approximately 10,000 Indians were captured at Kut.[39] Very few were to return home alive. Already ill, weak and dispirited few would be able to survive the long and harsh captivity as they were made to march hundreds of miles northwards towards the area of Ras al-'Ayn. One eyewitness account described how troops were falling out of the marching lines en route from sheer exhaustion and were left to perish.[40] Another recalled the appearance of sepoys involved in the construction work as that of 'animated skeletons hung about with filthy rags'.[41] While Indian Muslim POWs received preferential treatment and were sent to camps in Anatolia, Hindu and Christian POWs were stopped at Ras al-'Ayn, where they were put to work on the Berlin–Baghdad railway line where they had almost no shelter and bare rations to survive on. When winter set in the conditions became almost unbearable. Sarbadhikari wrote,

'That was our first winter in Turkey and we had no clothes to speak of; many didn't have boots... [The prisoners] would be taken to work barefoot on the line, in the snow. They would get frostbite at first and then the flesh would fall off and the wounds would turn gangrenous.'[42] It is not surprising then that E.A. Walker, a British officer, estimated that nearly 75 per cent of the Indian POWs who worked on the railway lines died in the first year.[43]

The experience of Indian POWs in Turkey also encapsulated a complex set of negotiations and relations with the British POWs who had been captured with them, in addition to their Turkish captor.[44] The loss at Kut only unleashed more brutally the notions of racial superiority that were perhaps not aired so clearly at times of victory. The siege had already caused fissures to arise between the British and Indian troops. Some British resented the Indians' dietary rigidness. Others suspected their loyalty and chafed at the special treatment the Turks began giving the captured Indian Muslims. Sisir Sarbadhikari in his memoirs describes such feelings being vented after the capitulation at Kut:

> The white or British soldiers are behaving very badly with the black or Indian sepoys; they're even beating them! They say that it is because of the Indians that they lost at Kut! It's unimaginably vile. The astonishing thing is that even when complaints are taken to the British officers, they do nothing.[45]

Even as POWs, the British expected imperial racial hierarchies to be respected by their captors. Major E.W.C. Sandes who was captured with the 6th Division at Kut recalled how as POWs 'our first business was naturally to get separate accommodation for the Indian officers... we explained also that Indian officers, in spite of the badges of rank on their shoulders, were always of inferior rank to British officers and were under their orders.' On a steamer voyage to Baghdad after the surrender at Kut, British troops were provided sleeping space on the lower deck while six hundred Indians were crammed on the upper deck.[46] Yet Sandes, like a number of other British officers, also insisted that British suffered more than their Indian counterparts. 'Our Indian rank and file suffered severely, it is true,' noted Sandes, 'but not to the extent of the British.'[47]

One can only wonder about the impact such behaviour and slights had on the Indians and if these caused the captured Indians to question their loyalty more strongly than any Ottoman-German attempts at propaganda. There is no clear answer, but Sisir Sarbadhikari's memoirs point to a greater political awareness of this inequality amongst perhaps at least a few Indians:

> Some funds have arrived for us from the Red Cross Society – 3 liras for the British, and one and a half liras for us. We all refused it... [But] After much persuasion... we agreed to take the one and a half liras. What we said when we refused the money was that white soldiers are paid higher salaries in India because they are serving in a foreign country and therefore have extra expenses... But that argument doesn't work in this instance. Turkey is not our country, just as it is not theirs... The differences and distinctions that have been created between whites and blacks in all things is deeply insulting to us. A Hindustani sepoy receives half the pay that a white soldier gets; his clothing and uniform is different too – the white's is better. But the white Tommy and the black sepoy both put aside their love of life to go to war, they both suffer equally – yet in the midst of shared hardship, everything possible is done to make things better for Tommy.

> Even his rations are different – Tommy drinks his tea with sugar, we drink it with jaggery. And what tea it is! Sacks of it lie in front of the store; people walk over it with their boots. If there's a canteen then we aren't allowed into it; only whites can buy from them... A lot can be written about this. [48]

Sarbadhikari's memoir is perhaps unique in cogently recounting these complexities of negotiating with the colonial master, but even more importantly recounts an intimacy built with another peoples, the Armenians, who at the time were bearing the full brunt of the Ottoman Empire's repression. 'We run into our Armenian colleagues every day,' noted Sisir at one point. 'They're in despair. But what can we do for them?' Another time he wrote, 'They have become like our own. I wonder, even if the Turks don't kill them, what will they find when they get home? Who will they return to? Who knows if they even have any homes left!'[49] Ras al-'Ayn was one of the key sites of the Armenian genocide and the Indians were not only a witness to the death and destruction the pogroms had wreaked but also built close bonds with Armenian refugees who survived and were living a precarious existence, worrying about yet another bout of bloodletting. Both Sarbadhikari and the British officer E.A. Walker recount the story of a small Armenian orphan, the sole genocide survivor from his family, who was adopted by an Indian sweeper, Jumman, and named Babulal. Babulal took to calling Jumman 'Baba' (father). When he was old enough, Babulal became a fifer with the Bengal Ambulance Corps and at the war's end accompanied his adopted father back to India.[50]

This sympathy for the plight of the Armenians did not preclude bonds from also forming with the Turks, many of whom were fighting in desperately poor conditions. The war was to be the death knell for the Ottoman Empire as the European empires gathered to divide its remnants, and more than a few Turks felt they had been pushed into a pointless war at the behest of their reckless leadership. For the Indians and the Turks in Mesopotamia, the absurdities of the war could not be clearer. 'We used to talk about our country, about our joys and sorrows,' noted Sarbadhikari about his conversations with his Turkish captors.

> One thing they always said was this: What are you going to gain from this war? Why are we cutting each other's throats? You live in Hindustan, we live in Turkey, neither of us have ever met, we have no quarrel with each other, but at the behest of a couple of men we've become enemies overnight.[51]

It would not be appropriate to generalize from Sarbadhikari's words about an Indian reaction to the experience of war and captivity. However, they do point to the ways in which the experience of war made at least some Indian participants question not just the absurdities of the war, but the hierarchies of the colonial system itself.

+++

Indian troops make their way from Baghdad to Samarra, a town further north, in a bid to consolidate their position of advantage over the Ottomans.

Tractors haul a howitzer across a river as the British troops advance against the Ottomans. The bridge had been destroyed by the retreating Ottoman Army.

The campaign in Mesopotamia made the building of infrastructure a necessity for the Indian Army. These pictures show a group of Indian sappers and miners bridging a river.

Indian troops board Bellums at Basra, 1915. The desert afforded little cover to advancing troops and also posed difficulties of transport and logistics due to a lack of roads or railways. However, even river travel was difficult, especially in the dry season when only small boats could navigate the waterways.

M 21

An Indian pioneer regiment lays sleepers on a military railway.

Indian troops aboard horse-drawn tram cars which ran between Baghdad and the neighbouring town of Kadhimiya, July 1917. By this time, the Allied troops had captured Baghdad making more conspicuous forms of transport such as these carts viable.

Indian troops cross the desert on horse carts. On the horizon, clear signs of battle can be seen.

An armoured Rolls Royce car on patrol in the desert.

Above: Indian sappers work at recovering Turkish war material from the Tigris.

Facing Page: One soldier is pictured preparing for a gas drill, while another is seen holding a spray nozzle. As the war continued, gas masks became more advanced and the one seen on the soldier here is much more sophisticated than the early iterations used on the Western Front.

Punjabi Muslim soldiers training behind the line at an assault course.

A platoon of the 1/2 Rajputs pass a heavy artillery battery in action.

A heavy battery photographed in the desert.

Clockwise from left: Indian signalers operate a heliograph; sepoys watch an anti-aircraft battery firing at an enemy plane; a Lewis gunner waits to put up a barrage for an attacking aircraft.

Indian troops guarding the Baghdad railway station.

Facing page: An Indian cavalryman in Mesopotamia shares his rations with a local peasant girl. The photograph featured on the front page of *Jangi Akhbar*, a propaganda newspaper distributed among Indian troops on the various war fronts.

प्रति मास में दो बार प्रकाशित ॥
मूल्य एक आना ॥

جنگی اخبار
JAṄGĪ AKHBĀR
जंगी अख़बार.

قیمت ایک آنہ
مہینہ میں دو بار
شائع ہوتا ہے -

ਜੰਗੀ ਅਖਬਾਰ.

ਮਹੀਨੇ ਵਿਚ ਦੋ ਵਾਰ ਛਪਦੀ ਹੈ ॥
ਮੁਲ ਇਕ ਆਨਾ ॥

३१ संख्या. | نمبر ٣١ | ਨਾ ੩੧.

ایک ہندوستانی سوار عراق میں اپنی خوراک بھوکی دیہاتی لڑکیوں کے ساتھ ملکر کھا رہا ہے -

ਮੈਸੋਪੋਟੇਮਿਆ ਵਿਚ ਇਕ ਹਿੰਦੁਸਤਾਨੀ ਘੁੜਸਵਾਰ ਸਿਪਾਹੀ ਭੁਖੀ ਪਿੰਡ ਦੀ ਕੁੜਿਆਂ ਦੇ ਨਾਲ ਆਪਣੀ ਖੁਰਾਕ ਵੰਡਦਾ ਪਿਆ ਹੈ.

मेसोपोटामिया में हिन्दुस्तानी सवार भूखी देहाती लड़कियों को कुछ अपनी ख़ुराक दे रहा है.

AN INDIAN CAVALRYMAN IN MESOPOTAMIA SHARES HIS RATIONS WITH HUNGRY PEASANT-GIRLS.

Facing page: Indian troops receive a dose of quinine to ward off diseases like malaria and cholera. These were major concerns in Mesopotamia given the poor quality of water and the abundance of mosquitoes.

Above: Indian stretcher bearers bringing in the wounded. The medical staff, especially during the first half of the campaign, was regularly stretched due to a lack of proper hospitals and facilities. The poor medical facilities in Mesopotamia became the cause of a scandal following the setback at Ctesiphon and the siege at Kut.

Ranks of Punjabi Muslim soldiers at prayer in the desert. The loyalty of Muslim soldiers was a constant source of concern for the British authorities running the Mesopotamia campaign. The soldiers had been asked to fight against their co-religionists and in defiance of the proclamation of the Ottoman Sultan (and Caliph) that proclaimed the war a jihad and issued a fatwa calling on the Muslims of the world to unite and to support the Caliphate above all else.

Men of the 45th Sikhs (52nd Infantry Brigade, 17th Division) marching with the Guru Granth Sahib to attend a Diwan, a Sikh religious ceremony, during the campaign.

5

Clockwise from left: Members of the Indian Porter Corps perform an open theatre at Kut; Indian troops headed by a bagpipe player and a drummer march to a forward area in the desert; Performers of an Indian concert party are pictured at the Royal Ordnance Corps theatre, Baghdad. Some of the performers, including the female impersonators, have their faces whitened with flour. A note on the reverse of the original photograph states that the performance lasted from 8pm until 3.30am.

VICTORIA CROSS WINNERS

The Victoria Cross (VC) was the highest military decoration for valour 'in the face of the enemy' awarded to members of the Indian Army during the First World War. Indian troops were not originally eligible for the Victoria Cross as they were initially controlled by the East India Company. Instead, the highest decoration they could receive was the Indian Order of Merit, which had been established in 1837. However, by the end of the 19th century, calls for Indian troops to be awarded the Victoria Cross had intensified, and Indian troops became eligible for the award in 1911.

KHUDADAD KHAN
129TH DUKE OF CONNAUGHT'S OWN BALUCHIS
1914 FIRST WORLD WAR
HOLLEBEKE, BELGIUM

FOR WORKING HIS GUN UNTIL ALL THE OTHER MEN OF HIS DETACHMENT HAD BEEN KILLED DESPITE BEING SERIOUSLY WOUNDED. LEFT FOR DEAD, HE MANAGED TO CRAWL BACK TO HIS REGIMENT DURING THE NIGHT.

DARWAN NEGI
39TH GARHWAL RIFLES
1914 FIRST WORLD WAR
FESTUBERT, FRANCE

FOR LEADING THE CHARGE IN RETAKING AND CLEARING ENEMY TRENCHES IN THE FACE OF SEVERE FIRE FROM BOMBS AND RIFLES DESPITE SUFFERING TWO WOUNDS IN THE HEAD AND A WOUNDED ARM.

CHATTA SINGH
9TH BHOPAL INFANTRY
1916 FIRST WORLD WAR
WADI, MESOPOTAMIA

FOR LEAVING COVER TO ASSIST HIS COMMANDING OFFICER, WHO WAS LYING WOUNDED AND HELPLESS IN THE OPEN, BEFORE BRINGING THE OFFICER INTO SAFETY UNDER THE COVER OF DARKNESS.

LALA
41ST DOGRAS
1916 FIRST WORLD WAR
EL ORAH, MESOPOTAMIA

FOR SAVING FIVE MEN, INCLUDING HIS OWN ADJUTANT, WHO WERE LYING SEVERELY WOUNDED IN THE OPEN BY DRAGGING THEM INTO A TEMPORARY TRENCH HE HAD DUG HIMSELF AND CARRYING THE MEN TO SAFETY AFTER DARK.

SHAHAMAD KHAN
89TH PUNJABIS
1916 FIRST WORLD WAR
BEIT AYEESA, MESOPOTAMIA

FOR BEATING OFF COUNTER-ATTACKS AND WORKING HIS GUN SINGLE-HANDEDLY EVEN AFTER ALL HIS COMRADES HAD BECOME CASUALTIES.

Gabbar Negi

39th Garhwal Rifles
1915 First World War
Neuve Chapelle, France

For entering the main enemy trench as part of a bayonet party, driving back the enemy until they were eventually forced to surrender. He was killed in the engagement.

Mir Dast

55th Coke's Rifles (Frontier Force)
1915 First World War
Wieltje, Belgium

For leading his platoon during an attack at Ypres and commanding various parties of the regiment until retirement was ordered. While retreating under heavy fire he helped carry eight officers to safety.

Kulbir Thapa

4th Prince of Wales's Own Gurkha Rifles
1915 First World War
Fauquissart, France

For rescuing three badly wounded men from German trenches while under enemy fire and despite being wounded himself.

Gobind Singh

28th Light Cavalry
1917 First World War
Épehy, France

For volunteering three times to carry messages between the regiment and brigade headquarters, a distance of 2.4 km over open ground, while under heavy fire from the enemy.

Karanbahadur Rana

4th Prince of Wales's Own Gurkha Rifles
1918 First World War
El Kefr, Egypt

For working a Lewis gun under intense fire to engage an enemy machine gun before assisting with covering fire in withdrawal.

Badlu Singh

14th Murray's Jat Lancers
1918 First World War
River Jordan, Palestine

For commanding a group of six other ranks and charging and capturing a small hill on the west bank of the River Jordan occupied by enemy machine guns and infantry. He was killed in the engagement.

Released Indian POWs from Kut al-Amara embark for home from Constantinople, November 1918. The story of Indian soldiers who returned from years of war often brutalized and suffering psychologically, is largely forgotten in the Indian subcontinent today, but these soldiers and their war-time experiences did have an impact on post-war Indian society and politics.

Epilogue

The war was over and though it did not happen in India, it seemed, from the talk of these people to have happened in India. And what was more, from all this unrest and shooting and what not it hadn't quite finished yet.

MULK RAJ ANAND,
THE SWORD AND THE SICKLE[1]

+++

The economic and social fixities of the country have been loosened, and India is changing in response to world conditions with which it has been brought into direct touch... The Punjabi particularly has travelled, heard and thought... He has been to other lands, and heard and seen and fought along with men of other nations, and had opportunities of measuring his courage, endurance and intelligence on many a battlefield.

EAST AND WEST, MAY 1919[2]

+++

The First World War began through the disintegration of European diplomacy and while it might appear that the war's most seismic impacts were on Europe it was just as important in reshaping politics globally. The war was a crucial moment during which anti-imperial and anti-colonial ideas gained traction across the world and this was true of India as well. As such, then, the legacy of the war for India's history was profound, not only in the ways it impacted Indians who had participated in it but also how it shaped India's national politics.

The local impact of a global war

The impact of the First World War on India was not just restricted to those who had seen active service during the war. The war years were difficult ones for Indians on the home front as well. Massive recruitment efforts, high taxes, war loans and a sharp rise in prices combined to impact the life of the ordinary Indian.[3]

Imported basic necessities such as salt, sugar, cloth, iron and steel, and kerosene became very expensive. Hoarding and profiteering only made matters worse. The distress caused by the war was becoming evident as early as 1914 and had become a full-blown crisis by 1917–1918. At the beginning of 1917, for example, wholesale food prices were 31 per cent above their pre-war level.[4] In Punjab, the heart of the Indian Army's recruitment base, food grain prices rose by 100 per cent between 1917 and 1919.[5] In 1918, a failure in the monsoon coupled with increased army demand for clothes

and food led to growing strikes and agrarian unrest.[6] At one point the Governor of Bombay, George Lloyd wrote to the Secretary of State for India, Edwin S. Montagu noting, 'Large quantities of valuable fodder are being exported from here to Mesopotamia by the Army... Luckily the Horniman Press have not tumbled to the fact that fodder is being exported while the Deccan starves.'[7]

Soldiers on the front in fact often received letters from friends and family conveying the economic hardships of life at home. From Ambala, Punjab one Barhan-ud-Din wrote:

> All over India famine conditions are severe. The rainfall had been insufficient. May God have pity on us, Amen. The scarcity of fodder is most greatly felt. Cattle are dying of hunger. In many places, no crops were sown, and where they were sown, they are in very ordinary condition.[8]

The war years also witnessed increased political turbulence with intensifying revolutionary activity, particularly on the part of the Ghadar movement (which was largely spearheaded by the Punjabi diaspora in the US and Canada and aimed to gain India's independence through revolutionary means). Military campaigns around the world had drained India of troops physically present in the subcontinent (at one point the number of British soldiers present in India was a mere 15,000). For revolutionaries, this signalled an excellent opportunity to exploit the weakness of British rule in India and their activities, particularly in Bengal and Punjab, flourished.[9] Importantly, the

Lord Kitchener examines Indian troops early in the war. The war was the Indian soldiers' greatest test till that point. Often, the performance of Indian troops won praise and admiration from British officers. Nonetheless, colonial assumptions considered Indians unfit for positions of command and these notions remained entrenched till the war's end.

rivalry between the imperial European powers during the war also helped in opening up arenas and networks through which rebellion could be spread at home. The work the IIC did in Berlin for the German government was just one example of the ways in which the diaspora sought to pursue its anti-British agenda. The British reacted to such activities with a battery of repressive measures that were given legal standing through the Defence of India Act, which was passed in 1915 despite strong nationalist objections. Under the act, local authorities had more power to prevent rumours, deal with incitement of 'hatred' and make wholesale arrests. Further, in certain cases, political opponents could be tried by a tribunal rather than via the normal legal channels.[10] Despite the increasing discontent among the population, the pressure of the economic hardships of the war and even revolutionary activities, mass discontent was not channelled and coordinated into a movement that could challenge British rule in India.

While the repressive nature of colonial rule, especially in Punjab, played a crucial role in containing the spread of revolutionary fervour, many people also felt that the revolutionaries were only making the already dismal living conditions worse.[11] Others felt that they would be better served by remaining loyal to the government. As one Punjabi wrote to his friend serving in France in 1915 about the trouble caused by the Ghadarites, 'Here in the Punjab dacoities have become very common. The people in their sin do not remember that the Government which protects us is fighting an enemy... In one week there were five dacoities. When will God give peace?'[12] The Chief Khalsa Diwan, the most significant Sikh charitable organization in Punjab at the time, believed its interests would be better served by the colonial state and reiterated loyalty to the crown. Priests of many Sikh shrines denounced the Ghadarites as 'renegades or thugs'.[13]

Even the more influential sections of society were reluctant to turn against the British. For the business classes, a major segment of society on whom the British relied heavily for support, the war had meant a huge boom in trade and industry, and they had little reason to challenge the status quo. As even the Viceroy at the time, Lord Hardinge, caustically remarked: 'The commercial classes neither hear nor see anything, and as far as I am able to judge, are amassing enormous fortunes... [Most of these people]... simply don't trouble at all as to what goes on in the country.'[14]

Most importantly, many nationalist leaders continued to strongly believe that support for the British war effort was the best route to win greater political freedoms. If, as the British claimed, the war was about the rights of peoples and nations then surely the British would have to hold up their end of the bargain if they wanted India's help for the war effort. Others held that Home Rule would be a condition for their full support for the war effort, but that this support from a self-governing India would therefore strengthen the Empire rather than fragment it. The 1916 Lucknow Pact between the Congress and Muslim League, for example, called on the newly appointed Secretary of State for India, Edwin Montagu, to institute Home Rule for India forthwith.

In limited ways, this calculation did pay off. The August 1917 declaration by Montagu, which stated in the plainest terms yet that self-government would no longer be a constitutional status reserved for white colonies, was perhaps a direct acknowledgement of the sacrifices India was seen to have made for the war. It was also symbolic of how the colonial relationship had changed in the space of a few years. Montagu in 1917 spoke of self-governing institutions but a mere five years earlier Viceroy Hardinge had written: 'I need hardly say that the Government of India have never for a moment thought that the evolution of this country could be in a sense of Colonial self-government. The idea is ridiculous and absurd.'[15]

Internationally, the American involvement in the war and the Paris Peace Conference pointed to a markedly different tenor in the rhetoric of global politics. At the insistence of the American President

Woodrow Wilson the Peace Conference accepted the principle of national self-determination, implicitly calling into question the legitimacy of the colonial system. These developments were not lost in India. The *Pratap* in an editorial on 6 October 1918 noted:

> India is exceedingly satisfied with the turn the war events have taken and wishes that the admirable principles which President Wilson has repeatedly enunciated and which have the support of the Allies are carried into effect. It is the duty of the Allies to establish that principle within their own dominions and England, the leader of the Allies, should extend that principle of India and Ireland.[16]

Despite such developments, once the war was over no particular efforts were made to move towards self-government in India. It was December 1919 by the time the Montagu Declaration eventually took some concrete shape in the form of the Government of India Act, 1919 which increased provincial autonomy. However, by this time the Act was proverbially too little and too late, especially given the Government of India's repressive tactics in a bid to maintain the status quo.

The sharpest instrument for wreaking such repression on the masses was the enactment of the so-called 'Rowlatt' Act in March 1919, which aimed at extending indefinitely the wartime restrictions on civil liberties through a system of special courts and detention without trial. The Act was met with near unanimous political opposition, channelling the economic frustrations of the moment. Tendering his resignation from the Imperial Legislative Council, Mohammed Ali Jinnah wrote to the Viceroy that by enacting the statute the government 'had ruthlessly trampled upon the principles for which Great Britain avowedly fought the war. The fundamental principles of justice have been uprooted and the Constitutional rights of the people have been violated at a time when there is no real danger to the State.'[17] For Mahatma Gandhi, the passage of the Act was a crucial determinant of the role he was to take in India's independence movement. Gandhi's *satyagraha* pledge against the Act

Above and facing page: Vintage postcards like these that were printed at the beginning of the war marked a high point in the celebration of Britain's sentimental connection with its colonies. While many Indians expected the war to further the cause of Indian equality, the immediate post-war years, with increasing state repression, riots in the Punjab and the Jallianwala Bagh incident, left such hopes in tatters.

wherein he vowed to 'refuse civilly to obey these laws' and 'faithfully follow the truth' marked the launch of his first mass movement.[18]

The uniquely Gandhian form of civil disobedience that involved the closure of shops and offices and demonstrations (termed *hartal*) reached a size and scale that concerned the British enough to crush them with ruthless repression. On 13 April 1919 a peaceful, unarmed crowd gathered in Amritsar's Jallianwalla Bagh was shot at under the orders of Brigadier General Reginald Dyer, without any provocation or warning, continuously until the army's ammunition was almost exhausted. With the province in turmoil, the Amritsar massacre had been intended to produce, in Dyer's words a 'moral effect'. Instead, unrest spread across the country, particularly in urban centres. British officials began to speak of the Raj being threatened by the most serious outbreak of disorder since the Mutiny.[19]

In addition to the disorder fuelled as a consequence of the Rowlatt Act, the threat of pan-Islamism that the British had been so worried about throughout the war finally took shape as a coherent political agitation in the form of the Khilafat movement. The rumours of a harsh post-war treaty with the Ottoman Empire helped rally Muslim sentiment and the movement demanded that the Sultan-Khalifa retain control over Muslim holy places, and be left with ample territory (including Arabia, Syria, Iraq, and Palestine) to defend the Islamic faith.[20] Gandhi, keen to build political networks to broaden the base and impact of his agitations was quick to reach out to pan-Islamists in an effort to incorporate their grievances into a larger national agitation. In 1920 an official alliance was struck between the Khilafat leaders and the Congress with both coming together in a nationwide non-cooperation movement that was marked by a remarkable show of communal unity.

The Chauri Chaura incident in February 1922 where a large mob set a police station in the town of Gorakhpur district on fire contravened Gandhi's doctrine of non-violence and led to the suspension

of the non-cooperation movement. The Khilafat movement, which had continued in patches, too reached its end with the victory of the modernizing Turkish nationalist Mustafa Kemal Atatürk in the Turkish war of independence and his subsequent abolition of both the Ottoman sultanate and the caliphate. The chaos of the immediate post-war period slowly abated, but the war and the politics it engendered was hugely important in determining the trajectory of Indian politics moving forward.

The war and personal politics

In addition to its impact on the national politics of India, at a more micro level, the war had a bearing on the quotidian lives of the millions of soldiers who experienced it first hand and were,

in fact, significant contributors to its outcome. It is almost impossible to document or distil into one clear, coherent narrative the precise manner in which the war impacted its Indian participants. What the soldiers and other non-combatants made of the war and how they were influenced by it was determined by very individual factors such as theatre of battle, religion, class, caste, and regional identity to name just a few. Despite these discrepancies in response there is no doubt that most of the Indian troops returned from the war as changed men. In the words of one British officer, the Indian soldier could now be called a 'man of the world'.[21] This worldliness also manifested itself in the politics of the retired soldiers. One of the most interesting outcomes of the war was the impact it had on the development of a political consciousness among some former soldiers and their role in the burgeoning national movement.

State paternalism had worked hard during the war to ensure that that there was a steady supply of recruits for the war effort and for the continued loyalty of these troops. Though Indian soldiers continued to be paid less than their

An Indian soldier exchanges coins with a man of the Greek Labour Corps at Salonika, Greece. Perhaps the most significant outcome of the war was the very personal impacts it had on the million and a half Indians who experienced it first hand. The war exposed the soldiers to new cultures, ideologies and ways of life that had a subtle impact on life in India in the post-war years.

white counterparts, there were pay and pension improvements during the war. A number of special financial rewards were also instituted during this time, including the coveted award of special land grants. At the end of the war nearly 420,000 acres of land were distributed to 5,902 Indian officers; 200 received special *jagirs* (estates).

Even after the war many serving and retired soldiers were keen to offer their services to the government. In Punjab, retired military officers formed associations that carried out unobtrusive propaganda. One pensioner in Tarn Taran, Subedar Ganda Singh of the 28th Punjab regiment, personally took steps to counter anti-government propaganda by organizing meetings of all 'retired Military Sardars, respectable gentlemen, and *Lambardars*' from neighbouring villages and collecting villagers to discuss and dispel unfounded rumours. On Ganda Singh's initiative village panchayats took on the responsibility of organizing lectures on the 'merits of the British Raj'. In another instance a Risaldar Major Prem Singh warned the government that rumours spreading through the countryside could not be countered through the press or by local officials. He recommended a regular 'lecture system' by persons carefully selected to tour the country. Not only was Prem Singh's proposal approved, he was appointed a 'lecturer' for propaganda work in Punjab. For his efforts Prem Singh was paid a princely sum of Rs.5 per day and also given allowance for an orderly.[22]

Despite these dispersed yet ardent examples of loyalty, the state's largesse had its limits especially given the enormous bulge in rank-and-file recruitment during the last two years of the war. In certain provinces, especially Punjab, which had provided nearly 60 per cent of the Indian combatant troops who fought in the war, coercive tactics had increasingly been used to fuel recruitment as the war continued.[23] These measures began to engender bitterness amongst sections of the local population. More importantly, when the war ended, the ensuing mass demobilization only added to the existent discontent, making many soldiers think their efforts had not been adequately rewarded. For a majority of men returning from the war there was no prize of land and no cash reward for their loyalty or bravery. As if to add insult to injury, these soldiers, often heavily affected by war trauma, were greeted by a lack of jobs and opportunity in a depressed economic climate on their return home. Dissent began to compete with loyalty as a characteristic that defined the population's relationship with the colonial state.

Mulk Raj Anand's novel *The Sword and the Sickle,* a sequel to *Across the Black Waters*, tells the story of the protagonist Lalu once he has returned to India after fighting on the Western Front and spending time as a POW in Germany. In the novel Lalu returns to India hoping, perhaps, for a grant of land, as he wants to start a farm in 'Vilayati style'. He is willing to stay on in the army. Instead he is summarily discharged from service. Anand gives us a sense of what this abrupt dismissal must have felt like for so many of the returning soldiers:

> It occurred to him that among the many thoughts he had thought since he left Vilayat, he seldom thought that he would be discharged from the army like that ... blind faith in the benevolence of the Sarkar had precluded the whys and wherefores. He had fought for the Sarkar, conscious that as a soldier he had no rights, but still instinctively hoping for a reward ... To be sure, Uncle Kirpu used to mockingly say that a soldier's honour lay in his right to obey, but he had never grasped the significance of this remark in all its reality and power. And now that his confidence in the good-will of the Sarkar was broken, he could almost hear the words of Barkat Ullah, the seditionist, which he had heard in one ear and let through the other, ringing in his ears.[24]

It is unsurprising that when the limits of the state's generosity were laid bare it often triggered insubordination amongst at least some demobilized soldiers. In this, their experience of fighting and interacting on an equal footing with Europeans during the war, as well as exposure to enemy propaganda may have played a part. More than a few men began questioning the preconceptions that they had so far mutely accepted as the norm.

For many Indian troops the war was an experience that broadened their horizons and increased their knowledge of the world. Sib Singh, an Indian POW in Germany, is one of the voices recorded for posterity in Berlin's *Lautarchiv*. In his recording Singh notes:

> The German badshah is very wise. He wages war with all the badshahs. A lot will be printed when the war is over. The Angrez is badshah in India and we did not know there were other badshahs. When the war began we heard of several badshahs. One flaw in India is that people are without knowledge, they don't know anything.[25]

Sib Singh articulates the harsh realization of the limits of their knowledge many Indian troops would have come to when confronted with a larger world. [26] As they continued their engagement in the war, amazement at what was different and foreign made way for a more nuanced notion of geography and politics.[27]

The Sword and the Sickle explores some of these themes as it traces Lalu's journey as he becomes more revolutionary and active in socialist politics. At one point in the book Lalu rallies a crowd by articulating his own grievances: 'I was demobilized without even the mention of a reward, just because I was a prisoner of war in Germany. There was no talk of medals or the promises of land with which they lured us to make shields of our bodies for the defence of their own lands. I tell you it was a deception of my comrades. It was a lie for which they died!'[28] While the book is indicative of Anand's own communist ideology, it does correctly allude to the ways in which the war gave birth to various kinds of political awareness across the country. For example, the events of the Russian Revolution that took place in the midst of the war did expose many Indians to the ideas of communism and was no doubt an appealing ideology for the revolutionaries and disillusioned alike. Tellingly, the Ghadar movement took a communist turn in the years after the war and worked to spread these ideas at home.[29] A character in *The Sword and the Sickle* presciently notes, 'the war has done this for us at least – it has created the conditions when all over the cities and villages of India are waking up.'[30]

Traces of Lalu can be found in the archives in occasional stories of rebellious soldiers. It is revealing that the post-Rowlatt Act protests were at their worst in districts like Amritsar, Lahore, and Gujranwala, which had borne the harshest brunt of recruitment.[31] Amongst the agitators in the wake of the Rowlatt Act's passage, for example, were four sepoys who were convicted of an assault on the treasury in the town of Tarn Taran. In another case, a mob at Wagah was led by a havildar, Sulakhan Singh, of the 54th Sikhs who had had till then an exemplary service record for 14 years. The government found it difficult to 'account for his behaviour'. In Gujranwala rioting escalated to such a level that Lieutenant Governor O'Dwyer had to respond by ordering aerial bombings and machine gun firing.[32] Significantly, just a year earlier O'Dwyer had boasted about how the proportion of soldiers to the adult male population recruited for the war had been forced up from 1:150 to 1:44 in a single year in the same district.[33]

Also of note is the story of Brijpal Singh, a kisansabha organizer and a sepoy attached to the 9th Bhopal Infantry who was arrested while addressing a prohibited agrarian gathering in Rae Bareilly district in March 1921 prompting a violent confrontation between the farmers and the police. When Singh was arrested he protested that for four years he had been a prisoner of war in Germany and even the Germans had not handcuffed him. He pleaded that he was willing to accompany the police without handcuffs only to be met by the abuses of the police officer thus causing the gathered crowd to attack the police with stones and *lathis*. Brijpal Singh was freed and only recaptured after police reinforcements were sent for. When he was sentenced to imprisonment, the judge noted that Singh seemed to have thought he was in the 'battlefields of France'. The comment seems to suggest how once the war was over the only remnant of that experience these former soldiers were allowed to hold on to was their loyalty to the Raj. There was no room for dissent and there was little recognition of the respect and equality that many of these men might have desired as a result of their service. These themes also played out in the clashes that preceded the final burning of the police station at Chauri Chaura. Bhagwan Ahir, a demobilized soldier from the Mesopotamia campaign, who was part of the protests, was thrashed by police officers who claimed he had no business to be so demonstratively disloyal towards the authorities.[34]

The stories of former soldiers turned dissenters like Brijpal Singh, Bhagwan Ahir and Sulakhan Singh today survive as mere footnotes in archives. What their stories do suggest is that, while not necessarily consistent, post-war dissent from former army personnel was important in strengthening new forms of identity and feeding anti-colonial nationalism. The historian Shahid Amin has noted, 'Military service overseas had a novel social and political impact on the peasantry recruited to the "Imperialist War", whether from UP or the Punjab. Demobilized soldiers in uniform, flaunting their war ribbons, figured prominently in many anti-police and anti-landlord battles during the course of a prolonged peasant movement in the Awadh districts.'[35] In Punjab, for example, large number of military pensioners continued to participate in tenant agitations and the Sikh Akali movement over the next decades to such an extent that it prompted the colonial authorities to reduce the proportion of Sikhs in the army. Their numbers decreased from 20 per cent in 1914 to 13 per cent in 1930.[36]

The words of one Indian veteran of the war articulate the ways in which the foot soldiers of the British might have become foot soldiers in the national movement against their former masters. 'Previously we remained satisfied with the existing circumstances. But when we saw various people and got their views, we started protesting against the inequalities and disparities which the British had created between the white and the black.'[37]

+++

Notes

Foreword

1 The Second World War was to produce many similar stories, most notably that of Captain (later Lt-Gen) Premendra Singh Bhagat, winner of the Victoria Cross, and his brother Nripendra Singh Bhagat, who joined the INA in Malaya.
2 Needless to add, I use the words 'India' and 'Indian' here to refer to British India, which included most of the subcontinent.
3 Cf *From Sepoy to Subedar*, trans. James Thomas Norgate, London 1873 (also pubd. Calcutta: Baptist Mission Press, 1911). The original Awadhi text has never been traced: it is said to have been dictated by Sitaram Subedar to an English officer. The Hindi writer Madhukar Upadhyaya has rendered the English text back into Awadhi in his marvelously evocative book *Kissa Pande Sitaram Subedar* (Saaransh Prakashan, Delhi, 1999): I strongly recommend it to anyone who can read Hindi (I am grateful to Dr. Ashutosh Kumar of Delhi University for bringing it to my attention).
4 Vedica Kant explains the 'martial race' policy on p. 27, Chapter 1.
5 The writings referred to here are Sisir Sarbadhikari's *Abhi Le Baghdad* (privately printed, Calcutta 1958; listed in the Indian National Library, Kolkata as: Sarvadhikari, Sishir Prasad: *Abhi Le Baghdad; Prothom Mahajudhher Khanikta*, Kolkata, 1958), and the letters of Captain Kalyan Mukherji, which figure prominently in the account of his life written by his grandmother, Mokshada Debi, *Kalyan Pradeep* (listed in the Indian National Library, Kolkata, as: *Kalyan Pradip, being the Memoir of Captain Kalyan Kumar Mukhopadhyay*, IMS, Kolkata, privately printed, 1928). It was Santanu Das's piece *Indians at Home, Mesopotamia and France 1914–1918: towards an intimate history* (which is his introduction to the volume Race, Empire and First World War Writing, Das, Santanu (ed.), CUP, 2011) that led me to both books – I shall forever be grateful to him for this.
6 My posts can be found at: http://amitavghosh.com/blog/?cat=12; http://amitavghosh.com/blog/?p=5402; & http://amitavghosh.com/blog/?p=4276
7 Painstakingly edited and published in a magisterial edition by David Omissi, under the title *Indian Voices of the Great War* (Palgrave Macmillan, 1999). My blog post on the book can be found at: http://amitavghosh.com/blog/?p=4180
8 The volume *When the War Began We Heard of Several Kings: South Asian Prisoners in World War I Germany* (ed. Franziska Roy, Heike Liebau and Ravi Ahuja; Social Science Press, 2011) presents a wide variety of these materials; it includes several voice recordings in the accompanying CD ROM. My blog post on the book can be found at: http://amitavghosh.com/blog/?p=4196

A Call to Duty

1 James Willcocks, *With the Indians in France* (London: Constable and Company Ltd., 1920), p.xviii.
2 David Omissi, *Indian Voices of the Great War: Soldiers' Letter, 1914–1918* (London: Macmillan Press, 1999), pp.142-43. Letter from Signaller Kartar Singh, France, to Kunar Khan in Ludhiana District, Punjab (Gurmukhi, dated 22 January 1916).
3 Hew Strachan, *The First World War* (London: Simon and Schuster, 2003), p.68.
4 Santanu Das, "Introduction", in Santanu Das, ed., *Race, Empire and First World War Literature* (Cambridge: Cambridge University Press, 2011), p.5.
5 Statistic quoted in the exhibition "Empire, Faith and War: The Sikhs and World War I" held at the School of Oriental and African Studies, University of London.
6 I am very grateful to Amitav Ghosh for allowing me to quote his translations of two Bengali memoirs, those of Sisir Sarbadhikari and Captain Kaylan Kumar Mukhopadhyay. Amitav Ghosh, "On to Baghdad: Joining Up", 15 August 2012. (http://amitavghosh.com/blog/?m=20120815).
7 According to government records the total number of Indian recruited during the war (up to 31 December

1919) was 877,068 combatants and 563,369 non-combatants to make a total of 1,440,437. This was in addition to the estimated 239,561 men who were part of the British Indian Army when the war broke out in 1914. (*India's Contribution to the Great War* (Calcutta: Superintendent Government Printing, India, 1923), p.79.

8 In the initial government tally in *India's Contribution to the War* the figure put forward is 53,774. Omissi quotes an approximate figure of 49,000 (Omissi, *Indian Voices*, 4) and Sumner a figure of 62,000 (*The Indian Army 1914–1947* (Oxford: Osprey Publishing, 2001, 9) The Commonwealth War Graves Commission in its 2008 annual report quoted a figure of 74,187.

9 Andrew Tait Jarboe, *Soldiers of empire: Indian sepoys in and beyond the imperial metropole during the First World War, 1914–1918*. Ph.D. dissertation, Northeastern University, 1 April 2013, p.12.

10 Commonwealth War Graves Commission, "India's Contribution to the First World War" (http://www.cwgc.org/foreverindia/context/indias-contribution.php).

11 Sumit Sarkar, *Modern India, 1855–1947* (London: MacMillan Press, 1989), p.150.

12 Radhika Singha, "Finding Labor from India for the War in Iraq: The Jail Porter and Labor Corps, 1916–1920", *Comparative Studies in Society and History*, 49:2 (2007), p.415.

13 Santanu Das, "Writing Empire, Fighting War: India, Great Britain and the First World War", in Susheila Nasta, ed., *India in Britain: South Asian Networks and Connections, 1858–1950* (London: Palgrave Macmillan, 2012), p.30.

14 Keith Jeffrey, "'An English Barrack in the Oriental Seas'? India in the Aftermath of the First World War", *Modern Asian Studies,* 15: 3 (1981), pp.369-86.

15 Santanu Das, "Imperialism, Nationalism, and the First World War in India", in Jennifer Keene and Michael Neiberg, eds., *Finding Common Ground: New Directions in First World War Studies* (Leiden: Brill, 2010).

16 Ibid., p.139.

17 Christian Koller, "Military Colonialism in France and in the British Empire", in Dominiek Dendooven and Piet Chielens, eds., *Five Continents in Flanders* (Tiet: Lanoo, 2008).

18 IOR/L/PS/18/D226: India and the War, pp.20-22; IOR/L/MIL/17/5/2383: India's Contribution to the Great War, pp.190-203; Santanu Das, "Ardour and Anxiety: Politics and Literature in the Indian Homefront", in the Great War 1916–1920' in Heike Leibau, Katrin Bromber, Katharina Lange, Dyala Hamza, Ravi Ahuja, eds., *The World in the World Wars* (Leiden: Brill, 2010), pp.346-48; Santanu Das, "Indians at home, Mesopotamia and France, 1914–1918" in Santanu Das, ed., *Race, Empire and First World War Literature* (Cambridge: Cambridge University Press, 2011), p.73.

19 Das, "Ardour and Anxiety", pp.349-50.

20 Ibid., p.349.

21 Das, "Indians at home, Mesopotamia and France", p.73.

22 A.R. Venkatachalapathy, "A great poet, a great war", *The Hindu,* 13 July 2014 (http://www.thehindu.com/todays-paper/tp-features/tp-sundaymagazine/a-great-poet-a-great-war/article6205029.ece).

23 Das, "Indians at home, Mesopotamia and France", p.73.

24 Judith Brown, *Gandhi's Rise to Power: Indian Politics, 1915–1922,* (Cambridge: Cambridge University Press, 1972).

25 For more on the issue of recruitment see Robert Upton, "'It gives us a power and strength which we do not possess': Lokamanya Tilak and Matma Gandhi as recruiters to the Indian army during the Great War," *The Great War: Regional Approaches and Global Contexts* (June 2014). Paper presented at the International Conference on the Occasion of the Beginning of the World War One. (Available at: http://konferencija2014.com.ba/wp-content/uploads/Robert-Upton-paper.pdf).

26 Das, "Indians at home, Mesopotamia and France", p.73.

27 Christian Koller, "Representing otherness: African, Indian, and European soldiers' letters and memoirs", in Santanu Das, ed., *Race, Empire and First World War Literature* (Cambridge: Cambridge University Press, 2011), p.133.

28 Max Egremont, *Some Desperate Glory: The First World War the Poets Knew* (London: Picador, 2014), p.206.

29 Omissi, *Indian Voices*, p.1.

30 Rough estimates based on Foreign Exchange

Rates 1914–1941 (available at: http://www.newworldeconomics.com/archives/2012/041512_files/Foreign%20Exchange%20Rates%201914-1941.pdf) and The National Archives Currency Converter (http://apps.nationalarchives.gov.uk/currency/default.asp).

31 Radhika Singha, "Front lines and status lines: Sepoy and 'Menial' in the Great War 1916–1920", in Heike Leibau, Katrin Bromber, Katharina Lange, Dyala Hamzah, Ravi Ahuja, eds., *The World in the World Wars* (Leiden: Brill, 2010), pp.93-94.

32 For more on the Martial Races Theory see Heather Streets, *Martial Races: The Military, Race and Masculinity in British Imperial Culture, 1857-1914* (Manchester: Manchester University Press, 2010) and David Omissi, *The Sepoy and the Raj: The Indian Army, 1860–1940* (London: Palgrave Macmillan, 1998).

33 Ravi Ahuja, "The Corrosiveness of Comparison: Reverberations of Indian Wartime Experiences in German Prison Camps 1914–1918", in Heike Leibau, Katrin Bromber, Katharina Lange, Dyala Hamza, Ravi Ahuja, eds., *The World in the World Wars* (Leiden: Brill, 2010), p.135.

34 Omissi, *Indian Voices,* p.20.

35 Ibid., p.26. Letter from an unknown writer in Punjab to a Jemadar, 34th Sikh Pioneers, France (Urdu, dated early January 1915).

36 Ibid., p.12.

37 IOR L/MIL/5/826/1/12. Reports of the Censor of Indian Mails in France: Vol 2. Letter from a sepoy of the 47th Sikhs in hospital, Brighton, to a friend in India (Gurmukhi, dated 14 December 1915); see also Susan Vankoksi, "Letters Home 1915–16: Punjabi Soldiers Reflect on Life in Europe and Their Meanings for Home and Self", *International Journal of Punjab Studies,* 2:1 (1995), pp.43-63.

38 For example, in France many soldiers requested language primers and newspapers. Some even picked up French and started incorporating French phrases in their prose or even occasionally writing entire letters in French. See Gajendra Singh, "Throwing Snowballs in France: Muslim *sipahis* of the Indian Army and Sheikh Ahmad's dream, 1915–1918", *Modern Asian Studies* 48:4 (July 2014), p.1031.

39 IOR L/MIL/5/825/2/222. Reports of the Censor of Indian Mails in France: Vol 1. Letter from Juvar Singh, Convalescent Home, New Milton (9th Bhopals) to a sepoy in Indian (Gurmukhi, date 17 February 1915).

40 Gajendra Singh, "The Anatomy of Dissent in the Military of Colonial India during the First and Second World Wars", *Edinburgh Papers in South Asian Studies*, 20 (2006), p.9; for more on pay and benefits for soldiers see also Dewitt C. Ellinwood, "The Indian Soldier, the Indian Army, and Change", in Dewitt C. Ellinwood and S. D. Pradhan, eds., *India and World War I* (Delhi: Manohar Publications 1978), pp.197-98.

41 Singh, "The Anatomy of Dissent", p.12.

42 Jarboe, p.117.

43 Ravi Ahuja, "Lost Engagements? Traces of South Asian Soldiers in German Captivity, 1915–1918", in Franziska Roy, Heike Liebau, Ravi Ahuja (eds.) *When the war began we heard of several kings: South Asian Prisoners in World War I Germany* (New Delhi: Social Science Press, 2011), p.26.

44 Gajendra Singh, "Throwing Snowballs in France", pp.1027-28.

45 The censor records are part of the India Office Records held at the British Library. These records consist of translated and censored correspondence between Indian soldiers on the Western Front and their friends and relatives who were either back home or serving in other theatres. The mediated nature of these records should be stressed. The letters were often written by scribes and whatever was written was expected to be seen by a censor. Furthermore, the letters that survive in the archives – while copious in nature – are only those that caught the censor's interest.

46 Claude Markovits, "Indian Soldiers' Experiences in France During World War I : Seeing Europe from the Rear of the Front", in Heike Leibau, Katrin Bromber, Katharina Lange, Dyala Hamza, Ravi Ahuja, eds., *The World in the World Wars* (Leiden: Brill, 2010), pp.37-40.

47 Omissi, *Indian Voices*, p.30. Letter from a wounded Sikh to his father (Gurmukhi, dated 18 January 1915).

France and Flanders

1 "Soldiers of India: Stirring messages from the King-Emperor," *The Times* (London), 3 October 1914, p.23.

2 Omissi, *Indian Voices*, p.43. Letter from Amir Khan, 129th Baluchis to his brother Lance Naik Khan Zaman, 84th Rifles, Rawalpindi District, Punjab (Urdu, dated 18 March 1915).
3 For more on the memorial, see Stanley Rice, *Neuve Chapelle: India's memorial in France, 1914–18* (London: Hodder & Stoughton Ltd., 1927).
4 Lt-Colonel J.W.B. Merewether and Lt-Colonel Sir Frederick Smith, *The Indian Corps in France* (London: John Murray, 1918).
5 IOR L/PS/18/D226*:* India and the War, p.3.
6 Corrigan, p.33.
7 Ibid., p.34.
8 George Morton-Jack, *The Indian Army on the Western Front: India's Expeditionary Force to France and Belgium in the First World War,* (New York: Cambridge University Press, 2014), p.140.
9 Mulk Raj Anand, *Across the Black Waters* (New Delhi: Orient Paperbacks, 2008), p.8.
10 There has been some debate as to the impact the presence of Indian forces had on the war in the Western Front. Corrigan and Morton-Jack argue (to varying degrees) that the presence of Indian troops was crucial in averting losses in some crucial battles.
11 Morton-Jack, p.154.
12 IOR L/MIL/5/825/2: Reports of the Censor of Indian Mails in France. Letter from Gulab Singh of the 57th, now in hospital in England, to Bhur Singh of the 25th Cavalry at Bannu (Urdu, dated 3 April 1915).
13 Corrigan, p.43-45.
14 Ibid.
15 Omissi, *Indian Voices,* p.125. Signaller Nattha Singh, 30th Lancers to Dafadar Wazir Singh, 7th Lancers, Force D, Mesopotamia (Gurmukhi, dated 8 December 1915).
16 Ibid., p.27. Letter from a Garhwali, France, to his father (Garhwali, dated 14 January 1915).
17 Trench foot was a particularly serious problem for soldiers during the war. The medical condition starts with chilblains followed by the feet becoming white, a loss of feeling in the toes and eventually the entire foot becoming numb. If the condition is not treated, the feet might develop gangrene and eventually require amputation. Trench foot can also cause damage to the nervous system that might persist even on recovery.
18 Corrigan, p.108.
19 Ibid., p.123.
20 Jeffrey Greenhunt, "The Imperial Reserve: The Indian Corps on the Western Front 1914–1915", *Journal of Imperial and Commonwealth History* XII (1983), p.55.
21 Anand, *Across the Black Waters,* p.91.
22 Ibid., p.87-90.
23 Omissi, *Indian Voices,* p.63. Letter from Havildar Abdul Rahman, 59th Rifles, to Raja Sajawal Khan Lumberdar (Urdu, May 1915).
24 Omissi, *Indian Voices,* p.195. Letter from Daya Ram, 2nd Lancers to Rohlu Ram, Ambala, Punjab (Urdu, dated 14 June 1916).
25 IOR/L/MIL/5/825/7/1084. Letter from a Sikh soldier to Mahant Partab Das, Patiala (Gurmukhi, dated 18 October 1915).
26 Omissi, *Indian Voices*, p.80. Letter from Santa Singh, Brighton hospital, to his mother (Gurmukhi, dated 20 July 1915).
27 Greenhunt, "The Imperial Reserve", pp.60-61.
28 Jeffrey Greenhunt, "Sahib and Sepoy: An inquiry into the relationship between the British officers and native soldiers of the British Indian Army", *Military Affairs* 45.2 (April 1981), pp.71-74.
29 Merewether and Smith, p.481.
30 Greenhunt, "The Imperial Reserve", p.57.
31 Omissi, *Indian Voices*, p.321. Letter from Lance Dafadar Dip Chand, 29th Lancers to Sri Kishen (Urdu, dated 26 September 1917).
32 Susanne Hoeber Rudolph, Lloyd I. Rudolph and Mohan Singh Kanota, eds., *Reversing the Gaze: Amar Singh's Diary, A Colonial Subject's Narrative of Imperial India,* (New York: Basic Books, 1999), p.202.
33 Greenhunt, "The Imperial Reserve", p.64.
34 Quoted in Das, "Indians at home, Mesopotamia and France", pp.76-77.
35 Greenhunt, "The Imperial Reserve", p.66.
36 Anand, *Across the Black Waters*, pp.76-77.
37 David Omissi, "Europe through Indian Eyes", *English Historical Review* 122: 496 (2007), p.373.
38 Anand, *Across the Black Waters*, p.59.
39 Omissi, *Indian Voices*, p.90. Letter from Saif Ali, France, to Kasim Din, 19th Punjabis, Seistan, Persia (Urdu, 17 August 1915).
40 Susan van Koksi, "Letters Home, 1915–1916: Punjabi Soldiers Reflect on War and Life in Europe and their Meanings for Home and

Self", *International Journal of Punjab Studies*, 2:1 (1995), p.53.
41 Omissi, "Europe through Indian Eyes", p.392.
42 van Koksi, p.53.
43 Omissi, "Europe through Indian Eyes", pp.384-85.
44 L/MIL/5/828/1/112. Reports of the Censor of Indian Mails in France. From (name omitted), Secunderabad Cavalry Brigade, France to (name omitted), Jhelam, Punjab (Urdu, dated 9 January 1916).
45 Omissi, "Europe through Indian Eyes", pp.384-88.
46 Ibid., p.395.
47 Anand, *Across the Black Waters*, p.129.

Face-to-Face with Blighty

1 IOR L/MIL/5/828: Reports of the Censor of Indian Mails in France. Letter from Ram Datt Singh, 71st Labour Company, France to Bhagwat Prasad Singh, Rewah State (Hindi, dated 16 March 1918).
2 IOR L/MIL/5/825/4: Reports of the Censor of Indian Mails in France. Letter from Lal Badshah, 40th Pathans, serving in France (Urdu, dated 1 August 1915).
3 Jeffrey Greenhunt, "Race, Sex and War: The Impact of Race and Sex on Morale and Health Services for the Indian Corps on the Western Front, 1914" *Military Affairs* 45:2 (April, 1981), p.71.
4 Jarboe, p.182. Sir James Willcocks, who commanded the Indian corps in France, estimated about 28,800 casualties among the Indian troops on the Western Front. After the war, a recount increased the figure to 34,252. Some regiments were almost completely decimated.
5 Omissi, *Indian Voices,* p.36. Letter from a wounder Garhwali in England to his elder brother in India (Hindi, dated 12 February 1915).
6 Greenhunt, "Race, Sex and War", p.73.
7 Indian soldiers were first transferred either to Brockenhurst, a small village close to Southampton on the southern coast of England, where two hotels had been converted into a hospital with just over 500 beds, or the Royal Victoria Hospital in Southampton. There were also small convalescent homes in coastal towns like Milford on Sea, New Milton and Barton.
8 Samuel Hyson and Alan Lester, "'British India on trial': Brighton Military Hospitals and the Politics of empire involved in World War I", *Journal of Historical Geography* 38 (2012), p.21.
9 IOR L/MIL/5/825/1/16: Reports of the Censor of Indian Mails in France. Note by E.B. Howell, 16 January 1915.
10 Corrigan, p.172.
11 Jarboe, p.217.
12 Hyson and Lester, p.21.
13 Joyce Collins, *Dr. Brighton's Indian Patients December 1914 – January 1916* (Brighton: Brighton Books, 1997), p.9.
14 Jarboe, p.217.
15 IOR L/MIL/5/825/2/211: Reports of the Censor of Indian Mails in France. Letter from Gulab Singh of the 57th in hospital in England to a friend Bhur Singh of the 25th Cavalry, now at Bannu (Urdu, dated 3 April 1915).
16 Hyson and Lester, p.24
17 Ibid.; Jarboe, pp.186-87.
18 Jarboe, p.182.
19 Hyson and Lester, p.21; Jarboe, pp.211-12.
20 Omissi, "Europe through Indian Eyes", p.379.
21 Hyson and Lester, pp.21-23
22 Omissi, *Indian Voices,* p.137. Letter from saddler Ibrahim of the 15th Cavalry [Lancers] at Brighton to Babu Rukan-ad-Din at Sialkot, Punjab (Urdu, dated 10 January 1916).
23 Omissi, *Indian Voices,* p.275. Letter from Jemadar Khisan Singh, 36th Jacob's Horse to his wife, Nabha State, Punjab (Gurmukhi, dated 6 February 1917).
24 Omissi, *Indian Voices,* p.54. Letter from Dafadar Muhammad Husain, 36th Jacob's Horse, England, to Dafadar Ray Muhammad Khan, 37th Lancers (Urdu, dated 13 April 1915).
25 Hyson and Lester, pp.31-33; Jarboe, p.214.
26 IOR L/MIL/5/825/2: Reports of the Censor of Indian Mails in France. Letter from Ragbir Singh, 59th Rifles, Indian Military Depot, Milfor-on-sea to Gajander Singh, Dhada, Kangra (Hindi, dated 8 April 1915).
27 IOR L/MIL/5/825/4: Reports of the Censor of Indian Mails in France. Letter from Naider Khan, in hospital in England to Zaman Shah, serving with the 57th in France (Urdu, dated 20 July 1915).
28 IOR L/MIL/17347: Censorship of correspondence to and from Indian Expeditionary Force in France.

29 IOR L/MIL/5/825/4: Reports of the Censor of Indian Mails in France. Letter from Duli Chand, Barton, New Milton, to Sepoy Chindgee, Village Burakhari, P.O. Charkhidadri, Dist. Jind (Hindi, dated July 1915).
30 Jarboe, pp.190-91.
31 IOR/L/MIL/5/828/2: Reports of the Censor of Indian Mails in France.
32 Jarboe, p.201.
33 Omissi, "Europe through Indian Eyes", p.379; Greenhunt, "Race, Sex and War".
34 Hyson and Lester, p.27; Jarboe, p.204.
35 Hyson and Lester, p.28.
36 IOR/L/MIL/17347: Censorship of correspondence to and from Indian Expeditionary Force in France.
37 Hyson and Lester, p.30.
38 Omissi, *Indian Voices,* p.119. Storekeeper D.N. Sircar, Kitchener's Indian Hospital to Telegraphist S.K. Bapat, Indore, Central India (English, dated 12 November 1915).
39 Jarboe, p.207; Hyson and Lester, p.26.
40 L/MIL/5/828/1/125. Reports of the Censor of Indian Mails in France. Letter from (name omitted), Pavilion Hospital, Brighton to Lance Naik Aman Khan of Bhamo Battalion, 12th Baluchis (Urdu, dated 19 January 1916). See also Santanu Das, "The Singing Subaltern", *Parallax* 17:3 (July 2011), pp.4-18.
41 Ibid.

In the Land of Hajji Wilhelm

1 IOR L/MIL/7/17276: Treatment of British and Indian Prisoners of War in Germany.
2 Lautarchiv (LA), PK 307: Sound recording of Jasbahadur Rai from Sikkim/ Darjeeling made at the Wünsdorf POW Camp on 6 June 1916. Translation from Britta Lange, "South Asian soldiers and German Academics: Anthropological, Linguistic and Musicological Field Studies in Prison Camps" in Franziska Roy, Heike Liebau, Ravi Ahuja, eds., *"When the war began we heard of several kings": South Asian Prisoners in World War I Germany* (New Delhi: Social Science Press, 2011), p.170.
3 L.A. PK 649: Sound recording of Chotte Singh from Kaudar, Fattehpur made at the Wünsdorf POW camp on 1 January 1917.
4 Jurgen K. Mahrenholz, "Recordings of South Asian Languages and Music in the *Lautarchiv* of the Humboldt Universität zu Berlin", in Franziska Roy, Heike Liebau, Ravi Ahuja, eds., *"When the war began we heard of several kings": South Asian Prisoners in World War I Germany* (New Delhi: Social Science Press, 2011), pp.187-206.
5 IOR L/MIL/7/17276. Treatment of British and Indian Prisoners of War in Germany.
6 See Philip Scheffner's film *The Halfmoon Files* (2007).
7 Ravi Ahuja, "Lost Engagements: Traces of South Asian Soldiers in German Captivity 1915–1918" in Franziska Roy, Heike Liebau, Ravi Ahuja, eds., *"When the war began we heard of several kings": South Asian Prisoners in World War I Germany* (New Delhi: Social Science Press, 2011), p.27.
8 Christian Koller, *The Recruitment of Colonial Troops in Africa and Asia and their Deployment in Europe during the First World War*, Zurich Open Repository and Archive (2008), p.20. (Available at: http://www.zora.uzh.ch/12048/2/Koller_Recruitment.pdf).
9 Ibid., p.19.
10 *When the war began,* p.143.
11 Jarboe, p.157.
12 Ahuja, "Lost Engagements", p.21.
13 Jarboe, p.175.
14 MSS EUR F143/75: Letters about the twice-weekly Hindi and Urdu paper *Akhbar-e-Jung*, with copies of letters written by Indian soldiers to the paper.
15 Jarboe, p.176.
16 Ibid., p.176.
17 Ahuja, "Lost Engagements", pp.22-23.
18 Hew Strachan, *The First World War* (London: Simon and Schuster, 2003), pp.98-99.
19 Ibid., p.99.
20 Sean McMeekin, *The Berlin-Baghdad Express: The Ottoman Empire and Germany's Bid for World Power 1898–1914* (London: Penguin, 2010), p.86.
21 Ibid., p.3.
22 Strachan, p.97.
23 Thomas L. Hughes, "The German Mission to Afghanistan 1915–1916" in *German Studies Review* 25:3 (October 2002), p.449.
24 McMeekin, p.91.
25 For more on Oppenheim see Lionel Grossman, *The Passion of Max von Oppenheim: Archaeology and*

Intrigue in the Middle East from Wilhelm II to Hitler (Cambridge: Open Book Publishers, 2013).

26 Heike Liebau, "The German Foreign Office, Indian Emigrants and Propaganda Efforts Among the 'Sepoys'" in Franziska Roy, Heike Liebau, Ravi Ahuja, eds., *"When the war began we heard of several kings": South Asian Prisoners in World War I Germany* (New Delhi: Social Science Press, 2011), pp.96-97.

27 For more on India revolutionaries in Germany see Thomas G. Fraser, "Germany and Indian Revolution, 1914–1918" in *Journal of Contemporary History* 12:2 (April 1977).

28 Liebau, "The German Foreign Office", pp.104-105.

29 Jarboe, p.134.

30 IOR L/MIL/5/825/1/120. Reports of the Censor of Indian Mails in France: Vol 1. Letter from a Pathan to sepoy, 55th Rifles, Kohat to a friend in the 58th Rifles, France (Urdu, dated 15 February 1915).

31 Jarboe, p.128.

32 Liebau, "The German Foreign Office", pp.113-14.

33 IOR L/MIL/5/825/1: Reports of the Censor of Indian Mails in France: Vol 1. Letter from Makhan Singh, a clerk in the 47th Sikhs to his sister in India (Gurmukhi, dated 14 March 1915).

34 Two sepoys belonging to the 57th Rifles deserted one night in August 1915, as did another pair belonging to the 27th Punjabis on 8 October. A group of at least 11 Afghans belonging to the 40th Pathans deserted sometime in late 1915.

35 Jarboe, p.127.

36 Ibid., p.138.

37 Ibid.

38 For more on the mission to Afghanistan see Hughes.

39 IOR L/MIL/17/5/2403. Nominal rolls of Indian prisoners of war suspected of having deserted to the enemy or of having given information to or otherwise assisted the enemy after capture.

40 Liebau, p.115.

41 Jarboe, p.233.

42 IOR L/MIL/7/17276: Treatment of British and Indian Prisoners of War in Germany. Extract of Summary of Correspondence contained in Report XXVI on the situation of British Prisoners-of-War in Germany.

43 IOR L/MIL/7/17276: Treatment of British and Indian Prisoners of War in Germany. Dispatch from Embassy of the United States of America, Berlin, 6 July 1915.

44 Ahuja, "Lost Engagements", p.35.

45 IOR L/MIL/7/17276: Treatment of British and Indian Prisoners of War in Germany. Mr. Sahai's report of conversation with "Exchange wounded prisoner" from Germany (Sepoy Ram Nath Singh, 9th Bhopal Infantry).

46 Heike Liebau, "*Hindostan:* A Camp Newspaper for South-Asian Prisoners of World War One in Germany", in Franziska Roy, Heike Liebau, Ravi Ahuja, eds., *"When the war began we heard of several kings": South Asian Prisoners in World War I Germany* (New Delhi: Social Science Press, 2011), p.234. The Indian intellectuals involved with the production of the paper included Ahmad Mansur, Taraknath Das, Virendranath Chattopadhyay, Chempakaraman Pillai, Bhupendranath Dutta, Shivdev Singh Ahluwalia, M. Prabhakar, Hardayal, Abdul Jabbar Kheiri, Abdul Sattar Kheiri, Abdul Hafiz, Acharya, Varma, Mitha Singh, Reinhard Kaundinya, Rishikesh Latta, Tarachand Roy (Liebau, "*Hindostan*", p.238).

47 Ibid., p.245.

48 Ibid., p.243.

49 "Indian troops eluded their Turkish jailers: Escaped from Constantinople and travelled over land to Afghanistan", *The New York Times*, 11 July 1915.

50 For more see Lal Baha "The North-West frontier in the first World War", *Asian Affairs*, 1:1(1970), pp.29-37.

51 Jarboe, pp.255-257.

52 LA PK 619: Sound recording of Mall Singh from Ranasokhi, Gurdaspur, made at the Wünsdorf POW camp on 11 December 1916.

Mesopotamia

1 Omissi, *Indian Voices*, p.144. Letter from Ressaidar Hushyar Singh, 16th Cavalry, Mesopotamia to Jemadar Harband Singh, 9th Hodson's Horse, France (Urdu, dated 30 January 1916).

2 MSS/ EUR/ C919: Typescript copies of letters from Capt Terence Stokes (d 1917), British Army 1914, to his father Sir Gabriel Stokes, written while serving with the 82nd Punjab Regiment in Mesopotamia.

3 These included 7,812 officers, 287,753 other ranks and 293,153 non-combatants.

4 For details on numbers of troops see Ron Wilcox,

Battles of the Tigris: The Mesopotamian Campaigns of the First World War (South Yorkshire: Pen and Sword Military, 2008), p.130.

5 Wilcox, p.2.

6 A.J. Barker, *The First Iraq War, 1914–1918: Britain's Mesopotamia Campaign* (New York: Enigma Books, 2009), pp.6-8.

7 Andrew Syk, "Command in the Indian Expeditionary Force D: Mesopotamia, 1915–16", in Kaushik Roy, ed., *The Indian Army in the Two World Wars* (Leiden: Brill, 2012), p.63.

8 Amitav Ghosh, "'On to Baghdad': From Calcutta to Aziziya", 16 August 2012 (http://amitavghosh.com/blog/?p=4440).

9 Nikolas Gardner, "Sepoys and the Siege of Kut al-Amara, December 1915–April 1916", *War In History* 11:3 (July 2004), p.309.

10 Omissi, *Indian Voices,* p. 160. Letter from Abdul Rauf Khan, 21st Combined Field Ambulance to Lance Dafadar Abdul Jabar Khan, 6th Cavalry, France (Urdu, dated 7 March 1916).

11 Amitav Ghosh, "Iraq 1915: A river of blood... why this bloodshed?", 23 July, 2012 (http://amitavghosh.com/blog/?p=4308).

12 Wilcox, p.14.

13 Charles Townshend, *When God Made Hell: The British Invasion of Mesopotamia and the Creation of Iraq, 1914–1918* (London: Faber & Faber, 2011), p.32.

14 Ross Anderson, "Logistics of the Indian Expeditionary Force D in Mesopotamia: 1914 – 18", in Kaushik Roy, ed., *The Indian Army in the Two World Wars* (Leiden: Brill, 2012), p.111.

15 Wilcox, p.15.

16 British and Indian rations were quite different, with Indian soldiers receiving smaller rations than their British counterparts. British soldiers received fairly large quantities of meat, bread and either potatoes or green vegetables, along with smaller amounts of butter, jam and tea. The Indian diet consisted primarily of atta, or chickpea flour, which was made into chapattis, supplemented by milk, lentils, vegetables, and assorted condiments and spices. Those who ate meat were given goat. By the last six months of 1916 more than 11,000 Indian soldiers succumbed to scurvy (Nikolas Gardner, "Morale of the Indian Army in the Mesopotamia Campaign: 1914–17" in Kaushik Roy, ed., *The Indian Army in the Two World Wars* (Leiden: Brill, 2012), p.397.

17 Townshend, pp.30-31.

18 Wilcox, p.71.

19 Gardner, "Morale of the Indian Army", pp.399-400.

20 Wilcox, p.70.

21 Each of the divisions of the Expeditionary Force had only 50 of the 125 beds authorized in their field ambulance sections while at the base in Basra there were only beds for 250 British and 600 Indian troops.

22 Amitav Ghosh, "'On to Baghdad': The Battle of Ctesiphon", 20 August 2012 (http://amitavghosh.com/blog/?m=20120820).

23 Wilcox, p.66.

24 Amitav Ghosh, "'On to Baghdad': The Battle of Ctesiphon".

25 Nikolas Gardner, "Sepoys and the Siege", p.310.

26 Ron Wilcox, p.70.

27 Amitav Ghosh, "'On to Baghdad': The Siege of Kut al-Amara", 23 August, 2012 (http://amitavghosh.com/blog/?m=20120823).

28 The troops were given two blankets, one to lie on and one for cover.

29 Amitav Ghosh, "'On to Baghdad': The Siege of Kut al-Amara".

30 IOR L/MIL/7/18848: Insubordination among trans-frontier Pathans (Muslim soldiers of Indian Army in Mesopotamia, Palestine, Egypt). See also see C.V.F. Townshend, *My campaign in Mesopotamia* (New York: J.A. McCann Co., 1920), available online at: https://archive.org/details/mycampaign00towngoog

31 Nikolas Gardner, "Sepoys and the Siege", p.315.

32 H.C.W. Bishop, *A Kut Prisoner* (London: John Lane, 1920), p.28. For details of the siege also see C.V.F. Townshend, *My campaign in Mesopotamia.*

33 Kaushik Roy (eds), p.413.

34 Gardner, "Morale of the Indian Army", p.412.

35 Nikolas Gardner, "Sepoys and the Siege", pp.315-18.

36 Amitav Ghosh, "Iraq 1915–16: The Siege of Kut al-Amara", 3 August 2012 (http://amitavghosh.com/blog/?p=4356).

37 Amitav Ghosh, "'On to Baghdad': Surrender at Kut al-Amara", 27 August 2012 (http://amitavghosh.com/blog/?m=20120827).

38 Omissi, *Indian Voices,* p.194. Letter from Karm Singh, Machine Gun Section, Sialkot Cavalry Brigade, France to Kalyan Singh, Jhelum District, Punjab (Urdu, dated 8 June 1916).

39 A wartime pamphlet published in Delhi estimated 10,486 Indian other ranks and 22 Indian officers were captured at Kut; a post-war estimated puts the figure at 9,300; Heather Jones, "Colonial prisoners in Germany and the Ottoman Empire" in Santanu Das, ed., *Race, Empire and First World War Writing* (Cambridge: Cambridge University Press, 2011), p.178.
40 Jones, p.188.
41 Das, "Indians at home, Mesopotamia and France", p.81.
42 Amitav Ghosh, "Shared Sorrows – 8", 5 February 2013. (http://amitavghosh.com/blog/?p=5558).
43 Jones, p.188.
44 Ibid., pp.175-93.
45 Amitav Ghosh, "'On to Baghdad': The Road to Captivity", 30 August 2012. (http://amitavghosh.com/blog/?p=4562).
46 Das, "Indians at Home", p.80.
47 Jones, p.187.
48 Amitav Ghosh, "Shared Sorrows – 10", 10 February 2013. (http://amitavghosh.com/blog/?m=20130210). Amitav Ghosh notes that Sisir consistently uses the Bengali words *gora* for to refer to 'white' soldiers and *kalo* (black) to refer to himself and other Indians.
49 Amitav Ghosh, "Shared Sorrows – 16", 3 March 2013 (http://amitavghosh.com/blog/?p=5692).
50 Jones, 187; Amitav Ghosh, "Shared Sorrows – 18", 10 March 2013 (http://amitavghosh.com/blog/?p=5696).
51 Amitav Ghosh, "Shared Sorrows – 12", 18 February 2013 (http://amitavghosh.com/blog/?p=5615).

Epilogue

1 Mulk Raj Anand, *The Sword and the Sickle*, (London: Jonathan Cape, 1942), p.13.
2 Ahuja, "Corrosiveness of Comparison", p.144.
3 Sarkar, p.168.
4 Judith Brown, "Britain, India and the War of 1914–1918" in DeWitt C. Ellinwood and S.D. Pradhan, eds., *India and the First World War* (New Delhi: Manohar, 1978), p.29.
5 Sarkar, p.190.
6 Krishan G. Saini, "The Economic Aspects of India's Participation in the First World War", in DeWitt C. Ellinwood and S.D. Pradhan, eds.,) *India and the First World War* (New Delhi: Manohar, 1978), p.162.
7 The reference was to the nationalist Bombay Chronicle edited by B. G. Horniman. Sarkar, p.169.
8 IOR L/MIL/5/826/4/513: Reports of the Censor of Indian Mails in France, Vol 2. Letter from Barhan-ud-Din, Ambala, Punjab, India to Risaldar Raja Firoz Khan, 34th Poona Horse, France (Urdu, dated 10 March 1916).
9 Sarkar, p.147.
10 N. Gerald Barrier, "Ruling India: Coercion and Propaganda in British India during the First World War", in DeWitt C. Ellinwood and S.D. Pradhan, eds., *India and the First World War* (New Delhi: Manohar, 1978), p.85.
11 Rajit K. Mazumder, *The Indian Army and the Making of Punjab* (Delhi: Permanent Black, 2003), p.236.
12 Omissi, *Indian Voices,* p.32. Letter from a Khatri Sikh, Punjab, to a relative, India (Gurmukhi, dated 30 January 1915).
13 Rajit K. Mazumder, "From Loyalty to Dissent: Punjabis from the Great War to WWII", in Kaushik Roy, ed., *India in the Two World Wars* (Leiden: Brill, 2012), p.465.
14 Brown, 'Britain, India and the War", p.33.
15 Ibid., pp.21-22.
16 IOR L/R/5/94/635: North-Western Provinces (and United Provinces) Newspaper Reports.
17 Stanley Wolpert, "Congress Leadership in Transition: Jinnah to Gandhi, 1914–1920", in DeWitt C. Ellinwood and S.D. Pradhan, eds., *India and the First World War* (New Delhi: Manohar, 1978), p.136.
18 Ibid., p.137.
19 Nick Lloyd, "The Indian Army and Civil Disorder 1919–1922", in Kaushik Roy, ed., *India in the Two World Wars* (Leiden: Brill, 2012), p.337.
20 For more on the Khilafat movement and pan-Islamism see Azmi Özcan, *Pan-Islamism: Indian Muslims, the Ottomans & Britain (1877–1924)* (Leiden: Brill, 1997) and M. Naeem Qureshi, *Pan-Islam in British Indian Politics: A Study of the Khilafat Movement, 1918–1924* (Leiden: Brill, 1999).
21 DeWitt C. Ellinwood, "The Indian Soldier, the Indian Army and Change, 1914–1918", in DeWitt C. Ellinwood and S.D. Pradhan, eds) *India and the First World War* (New Delhi: Manohar, 1978), p.178.

22 Mazumder, *The Indian Army and the Making of Punjab,* pp.243-44.
23 Tan Tai Yong, *The Garrison State: Military, Government and Society in Colonial Punjab 1849–1947* (New Delhi: Sage Publications, 2005), pp.98-140.
24 Anand, *The Sword and the Sickle,* p.26.
25 L.A., P.K. 610
26 Ahuja, "Lost Engagements", p.44.
27 Ibid.
28 Anand, p.52.
29 For more see Maia Ramnath, *From Hajj to Utopia: How the Ghadar Movement Charted Global Radicalism and Attempted to Overthrow the British Empire* (Oakland: University of California Press, 2011).
30 Anand, p.73.
31 Sarkar, p.169.
32 Mazumder, *The Indian Army and the Making of Punjab,* p.240.
33 Sarkar, p.169.
34 Shahid Amin, *Event, Metaphor, Memory: Chauri Chaura, 1922–1992* (Oakland: University of California Press, 1995), p.15.
35 Ibid., p.39.
36 Ahuja, "Corrosiveness of Comparison", p.144.
37 S.D. Pradhan, "The Sikh Soldier in the First World War", DeWitt C. Ellinwood and S.D. Pradhan, eds., *India and the First World War* (New Delhi: Manohar, 1978), p.224.

We would like to thank the following sources for the photographs used in this book:
British Library; Commonwealth War Graves Commission (CWCG);
Dominique Faivre; French Military Archives;
Garnisonsmuseum Wünsdorf; IWM; Mesut Uyar.
Map on endpaper: UK Punjab Heritage Association

First published by Roli Books in 2014
M-75, Greater Kailash II Market
New Delhi-110 048, India
Phone: ++91-11-4068 2000
Fax: ++91-11-29217185
E-mail: info@rolibooks.com
Website: www.rolibooks.com

ISBN: 978-81-7436-979-6

Editors: Priya Kapoor, Neelam Narula & Rayman Gill-Rai
Photo Editor: Saloni Vaid
Design: Sneha Pamneja
Pre-press: Jyoti Dey
Production: Shaji Sahadevan

Printed and bound at EIH Press, Manesar

Indian Army Campaigns during the First World War
1
2
3
4
5
6
6
7
8
9
11
12